TEACHER WELLBEING TRANSFORMED

PRAISE FOR *TEACHING WELLBEING TRANSFORMED*

Bianca McLeish has distilled multidisciplinary research to fortify educator wellbeing. In her first book, she has ensured that teachers learn essential skills and strategies within her pragmatic, compassionate approach. This book is a must-read for educators and allied community professionals when supporting our communities' schools.

Dr Tom Brunzell – Director, Berry Street Education Model (BSEM)

Teacher Wellbeing Transformed is an invaluable tool for any educator looking to protect their mental and emotional health while staying effective in their career. What sets this book apart is how Bianca helps readers understand the mechanics of their nervous system, empowering them to recognise the early signs of stress and burnout. Through thoughtful self-assessment tools and practical strategies, she encourages teachers to become more self-aware of their emotions and mental states. The strategies in this book provide real, actionable steps for teachers to regain control over their emotional health and maintain a sustainable balance in their work and personal lives.

Michele Adamson – Experienced Senior Teacher (Primary) and Author

While reading *Teacher Wellbeing Transformed*, I felt my daily struggles as a teacher were recognised. Bianca's use of reflective questions made me realise that my way of working is not sustainable and that burnout is inevitable if I don't make changes. Nothing is a quick fix, but now I have a renewed energy to prioritise my own wellbeing. Thankfully, the book includes strategies that I can start implementing today and, as Bianca reminds us, 'it's all about the small steps'. This book needs to be shared with all teachers!

Karissa Kirby – Senior Secondary Maths Teacher

As I read, I could feel my body becoming calmer – so many moments just made perfect sense. I was genuinely shocked that, despite all the professional development I've done, I spent most of this book thinking, 'Wow, how did I not know this?' I love how practical it is, with the exercises throughout guiding me towards a deeper understanding of myself. Every teacher needs this book!

Lisa Rankin – Experienced Senior Teacher (Primary)

Teacher Wellbeing Transformed offers a powerful blend of theory and practical strategies that truly get teachers thinking about their own journey and purpose. As someone who constantly operates on high alert, the techniques for completing the stress response cycle were invaluable. They showed me how to release the built-up tension from my day, preventing it from becoming emotional or physical baggage.

Holly Clow – Experienced Senior Teacher (Primary)

In *Teacher Wellbeing Transformed*, Bianca McLeish moves beyond surface-level self-care to explore the deeper impacts of stress, burnout and nervous system dysregulation on educators. Grounded in neuroscience and practical strategies, this book offers tools that are both accessible and transformative. At its core, it poses a critical question to education systems: why aren't we safeguarding the most valuable resource in education? This is an essential read for anyone serious about building school cultures where teacher wellbeing is not optional – but foundational.

Michelle Cole – Senior Partnership Officer, Learning and Development for Thriving Queensland Kids Partnership

Teacher Wellbeing Transformed addresses the ever-evolving reality that the teaching and learning space is getting harder for teachers each year. Bianca's style of conversational and informative writing invites the reader to feel like they are being heard and seen as they navigate their way through the struggles of burnout. This book not only provides tips and tricks to get teachers mindfully through their day but also empowers them to be informed about their body and mind.

Caitlin Cornish – Head of Department Student Services, PE and English Teacher

TEACHER WELLBEING TRANSFORMED

Break free from survival mode before burnout

BIANCA McLEISH

Published in 2025 by Amba Press, Melbourne, Australia

www.ambapress.com.au

© Bianca McLeish 2025

All rights reserved. No part of this book may be reproduced or transmitted in any form or by any means, electronic or mechanical, including photocopying, recording or by any information storage and retrieval system, without prior permission in writing from the publisher.

Cover design: Tess McCabe
Internal design: Amba Press
Editor: Rica Dearman

ISBN: 9781923403161 (pbk)
ISBN: 9781923403178 (ebk)

A catalogue record for this book is available from the National Library of Australia.

Contents

Introduction	Why are so many teachers stressed, burnt out and leaving the profession?	1
PART 1	SELF-AWARENESS – UNDERSTANDING YOUR NERVOUS SYSTEM AND RESPONSES TO STRESS	9
Chapter 1	Why do I feel so anxious at work? The impact of stress on your body and mind	11
Chapter 2	Why is it so difficult for me to relax? Discover how your brain and nervous system respond to stress	21
Chapter 3	I feel exhausted, so why can't I sleep? The impacts of a dysregulated nervous system	31
Chapter 4	Why am I so emotional and reactive? Developing self-awareness to understand your emotions and manage them more effectively	43
PART 2	SELF-EMPOWERMENT – TECHNIQUES AND STRATEGIES FOR REDUCING AND MANAGING STRESS	53
Chapter 5	How can I avoid taking work-related stress home with me? The importance of completing the stress response cycle	55
Chapter 6	How can I reduce stress when I never have enough time? How to manage your energy rather than your time	65

Chapter 7	How can I find time for myself when there is so much on my to-do list?	73
	Letting go of things you can't control and setting boundaries	
Chapter 8	Isn't it selfish to focus on myself rather than the students?	85
	The positive impacts of practising self-regulation and self-compassion	
PART 3	SELF-REGULATION – DAILY PRACTICES TO REGULATE YOUR NERVOUS SYSTEM AND PRIORITISE YOUR MENTAL HEALTH AND WELLBEING	93
Chapter 9	How can I stay regulated when I am faced with challenges every day?	95
	Create daily routines which prioritise your wellbeing and mental health	
Chapter 10	How can I manage stress when I am at school?	103
	Daily exercises to use during the school day to discharge excessive stress energy	
Chapter 11	How can I stop my mind from constantly overthinking?	111
	Mindfulness techniques to reduce feelings of overwhelm and help you relax	
Chapter 12	What can I do when I feel overwhelmed, anxious or have a panic attack?	121
	Techniques to stimulate your vagus nerve and promote relaxation	
Conclusion	Your wellbeing matters	131
References		133
About the author		137

INTRODUCTION

Why are so many teachers stressed, burnt out and leaving the profession?

"The demands on today's educators are unbelievable and not recognized. We need to be talking not just about the stress and mental health of kids but also about the stress and mental health of educators"
– Stuart Shanker

When Dr Rebecca Collie embarked on her research into teacher wellbeing, she was met with criticism suggesting that focusing solely on teacher wellbeing was inappropriate. She was urged to examine student wellbeing or explore how teacher wellbeing affects student outcomes, as the notion of investigating and prioritising teachers' own wellbeing was seen as selfish (Durham, 2024). Sadly, this perspective persists today.

It is widely recognised that there is a growing mental health epidemic impacting children and young people. Since the Covid-19 pandemic, there is a worldwide focus on addressing student mental health and wellbeing by integrating mental health education into the curriculum, providing access to counselling and mental health services, and implementing wellbeing programs. However, I am left asking: what about the mental health and wellbeing of teachers? Findings from the International Baccalaureate Organization study (2024) on teacher wellbeing indicates that teacher wellbeing significantly impacts student wellbeing and academic success. Despite the significant influence of teacher wellbeing, education systems often continue to place greater emphasis on the wellbeing of students, overlooking the critical needs of educators. To put it frankly, student wellbeing cannot thrive without mentally healthy teachers who possess effective coping strategies to support and manage students in a calm, emotionally regulated manner.

As schools are becoming more aware of this, they are looking for support from policymakers and educational leaders. Through my work with schools on improving student wellbeing, I have noticed an increasingly urgent concern among school leaders: how can we effectively support our teachers in safeguarding their mental health and overall wellbeing? This question reflects the growing recognition that educators need meaningful support to thrive both personally and professionally. So, I pose this question to education leaders and policymakers: why aren't we safeguarding the most valuable resource in education?

The need to prioritise teacher wellbeing and mental health

The media is flooded with posts about teacher burnout and increasing teacher attrition. Posts about 'why I left teaching' or 'why I don't enjoy teaching anymore' are all over social media, and the statement 'teaching is getting harder' is heard in staffrooms all over the world. There is a lack of resources, yet there is an increase in expectations, targets, mandatory reporting and challenging student behaviours.

The statistics on teacher stress, burnout and educators leaving the profession are staggering:

- The *State of the Mind Report 2024* conducted by Smiling Mind found that only 38% of Australian teachers feel that their colleagues are mentally healthy.
- *The Silent Cost: Impact and Management of Secondary Trauma in Educators (Interim Report)* (2024) reported that an overwhelming 75.3% of Australian educators said their work is emotionally demanding to a large or very large extent.
- The *State of the American Teacher Survey* (2024) found that when compared with similar working adults, about twice as many teachers reported experiencing frequent job-related stress or burnout, and roughly three times as many teachers reported difficulty coping with their job-related stress.
- The UK *Teacher Wellbeing Index* (2022) discovered that 78% of teachers feel stressed and that 79% of teachers experienced physical, psychological or behavioural symptoms due to their work.

But this is not just about statistics – this is about real people. I'm sure you see it every day with your colleagues – teachers are not OK.

Why I wrote this book

Over the past few years, I have been researching teacher wellbeing and intentionally observing and listening to fellow teachers. During this time, I have witnessed the struggles of highly effective, experienced teachers who are passionate about their jobs and love their students, but feel they have nothing left to give. As a result, we are losing some of the most amazing educators. Similarly, I see young, passionate preservice teachers, like my son's partner, who approaches her education studies with so much passion and enthusiasm. I do not want to see her bright spark extinguished by the immense mental and emotional demands required of teachers today.

In *The Silent Cost: Impact and Management of Secondary Trauma in Educators (Interim Report)* (2024), Dr Adam Fraser states that "Burnout, illness and high turnover of educators is not going to be solved by increased pay, work to rules or simple wellbeing programs. There is a need to view education differently and in line with current societal changes." I agree wholeheartedly! Supporting teachers to be mentally healthy requires more than just obligatory professional development sessions on self-care or designated 'Wellbeing Wednesdays'.

A new approach to improve educator wellbeing

While I don't claim to have all the answers, the stagnation of current teacher wellbeing initiatives signals the urgent need for a new approach – one that extends beyond self-care to address the deeper personal and systemic challenges impacting educators' mental health. This approach should focus on equipping teachers with practical skills in self-regulation, effective stress management and responses to secondary trauma, while also helping them recognise the early signs of burnout – before it takes a lasting toll.

Most educators do not receive adequate training or have a thorough understanding of how the brain and body respond to stress and trauma. Consequently, thousands of teachers who are feeling overwhelmed by the increasing stressors of teaching are not functioning at their best and feeling inadequate. I want to help teachers understand that a dysregulated nervous system may be contributing to their feelings of helplessness, powerlessness and overwhelm. My hope is to empower them with the skills to regulate their nervous systems and approach the stressors of teaching with increased self-efficacy.

How this book will benefit you

The aim of this book is to help you enhance your wellbeing and resilience by understanding the neuroscience and the role the nervous system has on your behaviours, emotions and mental health. Rather than be told that you should exercise or practise mindfulness, I believe you need to know *why*. You are an intelligent professional who has limited spare time. To make an informed decision about how to reduce your stress levels and improve your wellbeing, you need to become informed and empowered. In this book I will share evidence-based information, psychological tools and somatic practices to help you move out of survival mode. These actionable tools can be incorporated into your daily life to help regulate your nervous system and consequently regain the energy required to manage stress effectively, cope with the challenges of teaching and function at your best.

You need more than self-care

Most countries are becoming aware of the growing teacher wellbeing crisis and are responding with teacher wellbeing initiatives which promote self-care. Although self-care is necessary to maintain optimal wellbeing and mental health, I do not believe that it is the answer to teacher stress and burnout.

I think the problem with focusing primarily on self-care to improve the mental health and wellbeing of teachers is that it is often promoted as a self-care checklist, which often doesn't lead to sustainable change or noticeable improvement. This checklist can look a lot like this:

- ✓ Sleep well
- ✓ Eat a healthy diet
- ✓ Take lunch breaks
- ✓ Make time for relaxation
- ✓ Connect with friends and family
- ✓ Exercise regularly

The fact is that no matter how much you practise self-care and try to improve your overall wellbeing, if your nervous system is dysregulated, your system cannot heal without specific changes. For instance, if you are experiencing chronic stress and your nervous system is dysregulated, a good night's sleep will be physiologically unattainable until you can balance your sympathetic and parasympathetic nervous systems.

The need for self-preservation

This is why I suggest that self-preservation needs to come before self-care. Self-care is the practice of looking after and prioritising your own mental and physical wellbeing. Self-preservation is the preservation of oneself from harm or destruction.

Experiencing high levels of stress that force your nervous system to operate in constant survival mode can be incredibly destructive and detrimental to your health and wellbeing. Therefore, it is imperative that you understand how stress affects your nervous system, the techniques to restore a healthy functioning nervous system and strategies to ensure that you continue to manage stressors effectively. The more you understand what's happening in your body and mind, the more empowered you are to make change. Empowering yourself and prioritising self-preservation is essential, because teachers often fail to recognise the impact of stress on their wellbeing until it becomes overwhelming. Due to the constant state of stress that teachers are accustomed to, it becomes your normal – until you become unwell or burnt out. I know this because I've felt it myself.

My burnout story

A few years ago, I dreaded going to work each day. I regularly said, "I am going to quit", and I actively started looking for another job. I couldn't find the energy or passion to keep trying or care. I was:

- Frustrated by workload demands
- Exhausted
- Anxious
- Bored
- Overwhelmed by student needs (that I wasn't trained for)
- Not sleeping
- Regularly experiencing illnesses

I had wanted to be a teacher my whole life. My purpose had always been to help students reach their full potential and become the best versions of themselves, but I lost my direction and allowed my body and mind to become overwhelmed with chronic stress. I almost walked away from what truly inspires me because I was drained by constantly giving until all that was left were feelings of negativity, self-doubt, helplessness and cynicism. I had no idea at the time that these feelings were emotional warning signs of burnout.

Thankfully, one day, everything changed – but it wasn't my job. I discovered how to use tools and strategies grounded in neuroscience and positive psychology, which led me to an important realisation: while I couldn't control many of the stressors that come with education, I could take charge of my own wellbeing. The next few years at school were vastly different. While I stayed in the same school, had the same role, and faced the same demands and challenges, the key difference was me – and how I handled the stressors and managed the stress.

There were still many days when I felt disillusioned by policy decisions and internal systems. However, with a calmer nervous system and a clear mental space, I focused my energies on the students I worked with and the relationships I was building. I maintained my boundaries and did not let feelings of guilt and expectation take over.

Unfortunately, when you are stressed and disillusioned, it is easy to lose sight of why you wanted to be a teacher and feel like the only option is to leave the profession. If you are stressed, fed up, burnt out and ready to leave, I understand. But before you commit to leaving, I urge you to reflect on your reasons for becoming a teacher and consider trying some evidence-based techniques and practices that can help you manage stress and have the emotional space to enjoy teaching again.

How to read this book

This book is not a set of directions or rules to follow. It serves as a guide for fostering self-awareness, building empowerment and cultivating practical strategies that ultimately help you to:

- Understand the impact of chronic stress on your body, brain and nervous system
- Learn how to regain control of your time, energy and focus
- Discover strategies to become more self-aware of your nervous system states

- Learn evidence-based techniques to improve emotional regulation
- Establish daily habits to restore and maintain your physical, psychological and emotional resources

The chapter titles are written as common questions that teachers frequently ask. Each chapter's content delivers relevant information in response to these questions, thoughtfully addressing the realities of a teacher's role. It ensures that the strategies and techniques presented are practical and can be seamlessly integrated into the school day. Each chapter also includes thoughtful prompts for self-reflection, so you might find it helpful to keep a journal nearby as you read. Having a space to explore your insights can make the experience of self-development even more personal and powerful.

You might choose to start with a chapter title that resonates with you, diving into its contents first. Alternatively, you could opt to read the entire text sequentially for a more comprehensive understanding. The three parts of this book have been systematically structured. Initially guiding you to develop self-awareness, then equipping you with the psychoeducation needed for self-empowerment and ultimately providing practical tools to help you achieve self-regulation.

PART 1
SELF-AWARENESS

UNDERSTANDING YOUR NERVOUS SYSTEM AND RESPONSES TO STRESS

CHAPTER 1

Why do I feel so anxious at work?

The impact of stress on your body and mind

"You are not too sensitive, needy, anxious, depressed, reactive or co-dependent – your inner system is just trying to keep you safe"
– Jessica Maguire

A few years ago, a colleague of mine, whom we'll call Tracey, looked at me in desperation and mumbled, "Why do I feel like this?" A student in her class was displaying challenging behaviour and she had called for support. She was breathing rapidly and trembling as she explained that after many years of teaching, she had never felt this anxious and distressed. Nowadays, even minor changes in the school day made her feel overwhelmed and she often dreaded coming to work. She was irritable with her family and spent most of the night awake, thinking about school. Like many other educators, Tracey was experiencing feelings of anxiety and overwhelm as she attempted to navigate the unpredictable nature of teaching in today's classroom.

Reflect: Ask yourself the following questions to help assess your stress levels and nervous system regulation:

1. What situations in the classroom trigger a heightened stress response for you?
2. How do you typically react when feeling overwhelmed; do you withdraw, push through or seek support?
3. Have you felt emotions similar to those Tracey described?
4. How does stress show up in your body during the school day? (For example, tension, racing heart, shallow breathing.)
5. How do you typically transition out of a stressful situation; do you have calming techniques or recovery practices?

Our bodies convey sensations and emotions as signals from our nervous systems to our conscious minds, alerting us that a change is needed. If you're unaware of why your body is reacting this way, it can worsen your experience, causing panic and making you think something is seriously wrong. When you don't understand what's happening in your nervous system, it's natural to feel fear and a sense of losing control. This can lead to extreme distress and anxiety, much like Tracey experienced. However, it's crucial to remember that, just like Tracey, there is nothing wrong with you or your teaching abilities. Understanding the impact of stress on your nervous system – and the link between your nervous system and your emotions – is essential. Rather than blaming yourself for 'not coping' or 'being too emotional', you'll begin to recognise that your body is responding with survival mechanisms to protect you in moments of overwhelming stress.

Understanding your window of tolerance

Psychiatrist Dan Siegel refers to your threshold for stress as your 'Window of Tolerance'. If your window of tolerance is narrow, you are likely to be stressed more often, but if your window of tolerance is wide, you will find it easier to manage most everyday stressors. As Figure 1.1 depicts, your window of tolerance is where you can effectively cope with triggers and stressors, and regulate your emotions. When you are in this state, your body and mind feel relaxed and clear. Your nervous system is in a state of balance, enabling adaptive responses to stress and enhancing your capacity for emotional regulation.

Figure 1.1: Window of tolerance

HYPER-AROUSAL
You feel overwhelmed, anxious and out of control. Your body wants to fight or run away. These reactions just take over – you don't choose to feel like this.

- Running away
- Being in denial
- Quitting
- Becoming angry or irritable
- Experiencing anxiety
- Blaming other

WINDOW OF TOLERANCE
When you are in your window of tolerance, regardless of stress or pressure, you feel you can deal with whatever is happening in your life.

This is the ideal place you want to be.

| Calm state of mind | Relaxed and in control |
| Balanced and grounded | Logical thoughts |

HYPO-AROUSAL
You feel numb, frozen and spaced out. Your body wants to shut down. These reactions take over – you don't choose to feel like this.

- Becoming compliant
- Feeling empty or numb
- Confusion
- Feeling disconnected
- Withdrawing from others

However, sometimes you may become aware that your body feels agitated and your mind feels overwhelmed, or that your body feels drained and your mind feels blank. A real or perceived threat, excessive stress accumulation or traumatic experiences can disrupt your ability to remain within your window of tolerance, resulting in you being pushed out of your window of tolerance and into hyper-arousal (fight or flight response) or hypo-arousal (shutdown response).

As indicated in Figure 1.1, experiencing some of the following physical, behavioural, cognitive or emotional symptoms may indicate that you have been pushed out of your window of tolerance and into hyper-arousal or hypo-arousal:

- You're constantly on edge and overwhelmed.
- You're frequently snappy and irritable.
- You experience fatigue and sleep problems.
- You are having attention and concentration problems.
- You're highly sensitive to sensory stimuli.
- You regularly experience body aches and pains or illnesses.
- You withdraw from others and feel disconnected.
- You have trouble making decisions and feel confused.

Remaining in your window of tolerance requires a healthy nervous system which has the ability to return to calm after experiencing stress. Certain experiences can shrink your window of tolerance, leading to challenges in remaining calm and triggering either the fight or flight response or an involuntary shutdown, commonly referred to as 'the freeze response', during stressful situations. A pressing concern in this context is the ongoing exposure teachers face to disruptive student behaviours, including aggression, defiance, violence and threats.

Long-term impacts of managing challenging student behaviours

There is mounting evidence of a rise in teachers grappling with anxiety, depression, trauma and burnout. Recent research suggests that this surge is linked to the immense difficulty of managing unpredictable and challenging behaviours in students impacted by trauma or mental health conditions. For many of you, these realities may feel all too familiar, requiring no further validation from research. You are likely deeply attuned to the challenges teachers and leaders encounter, making it easy to connect with the perspectives shared by the following educators during researcher interviews:

> "I have been hit, I have been kicked, I have had a child bite my arm, swearing, you name it, it's happened. You're not just stressed about that child but for all the other children in the room as well" – anonymous teacher (O'Flaherty, 2024).

> "It changes from year to year. Last year I had a student who was agitated, violent, negative and angry literally every day. His trauma impacted on me in a major way. I was crying myself to sleep at night. This year I no longer have that student and I'm generally relaxed and on an even keel" – anonymous teacher (The Energy Factory Pty Ltd & Deakin University, 2024).

In her book *15-Minute Focus: Regulation and Co-Regulation*, Ginger Healy (2023) states that when a student experiences dysregulation, their teacher will also experience a stress response. Time and again, teachers are unconsciously triggered by challenging student behaviour which activates the stress response. Even though you may consciously understand that a student's behaviour is not a direct threat, your stress response still prepares your body to react and address the unpredictable situation.

Take a moment to think about how many times a day you encounter students with complex or challenging behaviours that might push you beyond your window of tolerance. The number is likely significant, and each interaction with a dysregulated student triggers a stress response. Over time, this can lead to exhaustion as your stress response becomes heightened, working overtime to protect you. More concerning, however, is the impact of prolonged exposure to frequent interactions with one or more dysregulated students, which may unknowingly keep you in a state of hyper-arousal and survival mode for extended periods.

Stress and trauma

The cumulative wear and tear on the body and brain due to ongoing stress, known as allostatic load, narrows your window of tolerance. This means that you have a smaller range of emotional arousal you can comfortably experience before becoming dysregulated. Stressors that you may have previously managed effectively can begin to feel threatening, resulting in symptoms such as anxiety, hypervigilance and difficulty relaxing. Trauma can play a significant role in narrowing your window of tolerance, further increasing anxiety levels. It's important to understand that trauma is deeply subjective – what feels traumatic for one person may not for another. For instance, while one teacher might only feel annoyed when a student swears or yells, another may find the same behaviour profoundly traumatic due to personal history, reacting by shutting down or becoming angry.

Jessica Maguire, in her book *The Nervous System Reset* (2024), emphasises this nuance, stating, "Trauma is not about a past event, but about our present experience and the reaction we're still having in our brain and our body today." This highlights why physical and emotional reactions to student behaviour might sometimes seem exaggerated, as the brain perceives threats and triggers protective mechanisms rooted in past classroom experiences. Consequently, this dysregulated nervous system response, coupled with heightened arousal, can lead to burnout.

Burnout

The World Health Organization (2019) defines burnout as a syndrome resulting from chronic workplace stress that hasn't been successfully managed, characterised by feelings of energy depletion or exhaustion, increased mental distance from one's job and reduced professional efficacy. Specifically, I define teacher burnout as a prolonged state of chronic stress, evolving into a persistent condition where an educator has exhausted the personal and professional resources to do their job effectively. Table 1 outlines the key symptoms commonly associated with teacher burnout.

Table 1: Key symptoms associated with teacher burnout

SYMPTOMS OF TEACHER BURNOUT	
• Feeling a loss of passion or motivation for teaching	• Experiencing emotional instability, such as irritability, anger or sadness
• Struggling to complete routine or basic tasks, like preparing lesson plans	• Reduced productivity and feelings of apathy, low self-worth or hopelessness
• Emotionally distancing yourself from colleagues and students	• Feeling emotionally flat or disconnected

Thankfully, burnout is not irreversible – you can rewire your brain by developing emotional regulation skills which increases your capacity to tolerate distress. The first step to developing emotional regulation is becoming aware of your physical and emotional responses and notice when they are occurring.

ACTIVITY 1: Checking in with yourself

Before you read on, I want you to take a moment to check in with yourself. How often do you experience the following physical and emotional responses? Take some time to reflect and tick the boxes which are appropriate to you.

Physical responses	Rarely	Sometimes	Often
Tension in muscles			
Rapid or shallow breathing			
Headaches			
Crying			
Restless/on edge			
Racing thoughts			
Fatigue			
Sleep difficulties			
Digestive issues			
Fast speech			
Low motivation			
Chest pains			
Recurrent illness			
Body aches and pains			

Emotional responses	Rarely	Sometimes	Often
Anger			
Shame/embarrassment			
Anxiety			
Irritability			
Empathy			
Overwhelmed			
Defensiveness			
Depressed			
Helplessness			
Excited			
Confused			
Stressed			
Grateful			

What is your body trying to tell you?

Upon reflection, were you already aware of these physical and emotional responses, or did it surprise you to recognise how frequently you experience them? It has become increasingly common for me to hear about teachers' struggles with health issues such as shingles, migraines, irritable bowel syndrome, vertigo and back pain. Despite sharing the high levels of stress they're facing, not many of them recognised stress as a contributing factor to these physical responses.

Given that the International Baccalaureate Organization (2024) found teachers to experience some of the highest levels of occupational stress and burnout compared to other professions, it is unsurprising that stress is taking a significant toll on the physical health of teachers. Research by Cavallari et al. (2024) identified that stress impacts health behaviours and immune function, making teachers more vulnerable to conditions like migraines, gastrointestinal issues and chronic fatigue. Additionally, this study highlighted that prolonged stress among educators can lead to physical health issues such as poor sleep, physical exhaustion and susceptibility to illnesses.

These physical health issues and emotional responses are your body's way of warning you before burnout occurs. The problem is that you may not be listening. At times we become disconnected from our bodies, as we are too busy in our heads trying to plan and control every situation – including our health and wellbeing. When we notice discomfort, pain, fatigue or muscle tension, we often try to fix the 'problem' with medication (so that we can keep going) or attempt to ignore the symptoms altogether. In their book *Burnout: The Secret to Unlocking the Stress Cycle* (2019), Emily and Amelia Nagoski explain that for some people, it's been so long since they've listened to their bodies that they no longer understand what their body is trying to tell them. Accordingly, Part 1 of my book is dedicated to fostering self-awareness – helping you recognise your emotions and physical sensations. By deepening this understanding, it equips you with the tools to manage stress more efficiently and recover from burnout more quickly. With this knowledge, you can develop effective tools to better manage anxiety, fear and overwhelm, while adopting practices that calm and nurture your body.

Reflect: **Ask yourself the following questions to explore your emotions, physical responses and wellbeing when working with students who have complex needs and challenging behaviours:**

1. **How do you feel when managing students with complex needs or behavioural challenges?**
2. **Do you ever experience self-doubt or guilt when handling student behaviour? How do you navigate those feelings?**
3. **Are there specific student behaviours or triggers that cause noticeable physical reactions?**

4. What aspects of your role feel most emotionally draining or exhausting?
5. What support systems (colleagues, leadership, mental health professionals) do you rely on when feeling overwhelmed?
6. How do you currently manage stress and prevent burnout?

CHAPTER SUMMARY

- Our nervous systems communicate with our minds through physical sensations and emotions, which act as alerts that something needs attention.
- Misinterpreting body reactions can escalate panic, distress and anxiety. Recognising these survival mechanisms helps to reduce fear and foster control.
- Our window of tolerance describes the range within which we can effectively manage stress. A wide window allows for calm, emotional regulation; a narrow one leads to frequent distress.
- Signs of being pushed out of your window of tolerance include fatigue, irritability, difficulty concentrating, physical ailments and withdrawal.
- Persistent stress and traumatic experiences narrow your window of tolerance, triggering hyper-arousal (fight or flight) or hypo-arousal (shutdown) responses.
- Chronic stress, such as prolonged exposure to disruptive student behaviours, undermine emotional and physical resilience, contributing to burnout and a diminished capacity for adaptive coping.

CHAPTER 2

Why is it so difficult for me to relax?

Discover how your brain and nervous system respond to stress

"The great thing, then, in all education, is to make our nervous system our ally instead of our enemy" – William James

Stress is something that is frequently talked about within schools and education systems, but we rarely speak about the bodily system associated with stress – the nervous system. We talk about self-care, the importance of sleep and reducing workload, but no one is talking to teachers about what is happening in the brain to influence emotional regulation. Although you do not need a complex, scientific understanding of the neuroscience, it is empowering (and even life-changing) to recognise that the vital functions of the body are regulated by the autonomic nervous system and influence other aspects of ourselves, including our cognitive and emotional experiences. Therefore, by becoming familiar with your brain and nervous system states, you can increase your stress resilience.

The autonomic nervous system

Every human being has an autonomic nervous system (ANS). The ANS has two main parts: the sympathetic nervous system (SNS) and the parasympathetic nervous system (PNS), which are designed to work in balance to regulate the involuntary physiological processes occurring during cycles of activation and rest.

Figure 2.1: Balancing the nervous system

BALANCE IS KEY

Sympathetic Nervous System (Accelerator)	Parasympathetic Nervous System (Brake)
• Fight or flight response	• Relaxation response
• Energy mobilised	• Energy conserved
• Survival and protection	• Relaxed and safe

Sympathetic nervous system (stress response – mobilisation)

The SNS activates your body to either fight or flee from a threatening situation. Millions of years ago, this survival response was designed to protect humans from the real-life threat of predators. If a lion appeared, the brain's alert system was triggered, which sent signals to the nervous system and propelled the body into action to fight the lion or run away to safety.

Although we are not threated by lions today, your body is often set off inappropriately by situations that you perceive as stressful or threatening. Reporting deadlines, challenging student behaviours, parental expectations or increased workload can all activate your stress response in the same way. In response to these 'stressful situations', your body prepares you by increasing your heart rate, blood pressure and respiration rate. This maximises the amount of oxygen supplied to the muscles, helping you to either fight or flee from the situation.

Parasympathetic nervous system (relaxation response – rest and digest)

The PNS is designed to activate when the brain no longer perceives threat and feels that it is a safe time to rest, restore and repair the system. It works to balance out the stress hormones and essentially helps to restore a sense of calm and connectedness to the world. The PNS conserves energy use and keeps the internal systems of the body continually regulated. You will see in Figure 2.2 that the PNS is shown to have two branches: the ventral vagal state and the dorsal vagal state. These branches refer to the two sides of the vagus nerve – a cranial nerve which sends messages between the brain and body and plays a vital role in your PNS. When the vagus nerve is activated, it sends a signal to slow your heart rate and lower your blood pressure, telling your body it's time to relax.

Figure 2.2: Parts of the autonomic nervous system

```
                    AUTONOMIC NERVOUS SYSTEM
                    ┌──────────┴──────────┐
          Sympathetic Nervous System   Parasympathetic Nervous System
            ┌────────┴────────┐           ┌────────┴────────┐
          Fight             Flight    Ventral Vagal     Dorsal Vagal
                                           │                  │
                                      Rest & Digest/       Freeze
                                      Calm & Connected
```

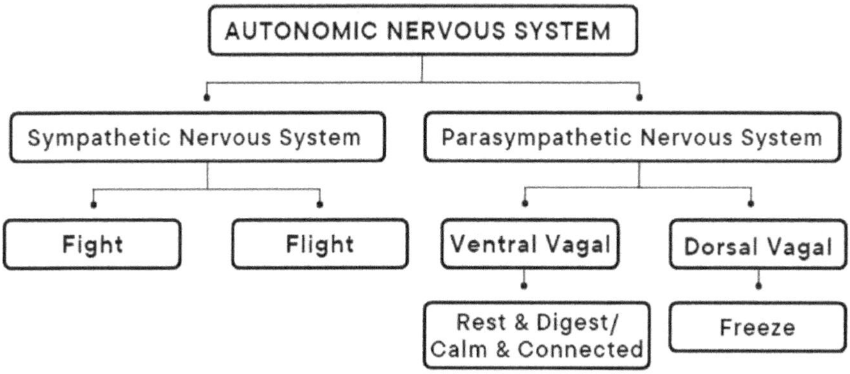

Polyvagal Theory

Over the past decade, Stephen Porges has expanded the traditional understanding of the ANS, which was previously thought to operate in two primary states: *fight or flight* and *rest and digest*. His research introduces a more nuanced perspective, proposing that the ANS functions through three adaptive states, each playing a crucial role in shaping daily behaviour and mental health. In *The Vagus Nerve Reset* (2023), Anna Ferguson explains that these three innate adaptive responses are essential for survival – one ensures safety, one reacts to danger and one responds to extreme threats. The three states of Polyvagal Theory are:

1. **Relaxed (PNS ventral vagal pathway)**
   In this state, our sensory system has not identified threats and consequently we feel safe. We can emotionally regulate, problem-solve and are seeking connection with others.

2. **Mobilisation (SNS)**
   In this state, our sensory system has identified threats and we are feeling anxious and fearful. We are primed for survival and action – fight or flight – and we have increased levels of cortisol and adrenaline running through our bodies.

3. **Immobilisation/shutdown (PNS dorsal vagal pathway)**
   In this state, our sensory system has identified threats and we freeze because we feel powerless to respond. We go into shutdown mode when faced with chronic stress or when the body and mind become overloaded and overwhelmed. Our nervous system fails to regulate bodily organs or successfully manage social relationships.

To simplify the science, we can use an analogy that compares the ANS to a car. The SNS acts as the accelerator, generating energy and driving action forward. In contrast, the PNS – specifically the ventral vagal pathway – functions like the brakes, slowing things down and promoting balance. When the parasympathetic dorsal vagal pathway is activated, it can feel like the handbrake is engaged, leaving the body and mind stuck in a state of shutdown or freeze mode, unable to move forward.

Which response state is better?

Each of our survival states serves a vital function, and no single state is inherently better than another. The ventral vagal state – characterised by relaxation and social engagement – is ideal for teaching, as it fosters positive relationships and meaningful connections with students and colleagues. However, in moments requiring swift action, such as a fire drill, the SNS's mobilised state is essential for helping teachers ensure student safety. In more extreme situations, like a lockdown due to a threat, the dorsal vagal shutdown response may become necessary, allowing the body to conserve energy and minimise risk. Understanding how these states function helps us adapt to different circumstances while prioritising wellbeing and safety.

Response states are hierarchical and sequential

Neuroception determines the three response states by assessing cues of safety or danger in our environment. Think of neuroception as your body's internal smoke detector, constantly scanning for safety and danger cues using all your senses to instantly and unconsciously determine if the environment is safe. Neuroception plays a crucial role in how we interact with and respond to our surroundings, ultimately determining the sequence and hierarchy of our response states.

Figure 2.3 illustrates how a teacher might adapt through the response states hierarchy based on neuroception. When no danger is detected, she is in a ventral vagal (PNS) state. In this social engagement state, she easily connects with students and is relational in her manner. However, when a threat or danger is perceived, the social engagement system becomes overwhelmed and depleted, moving down the hierarchy into the SNS. In this state, she cannot focus on connection, as she is anxious and trying to think of possible actions to ensure the safety of herself and her students. If the teacher remains in this heightened state of fight or flight for an extended period without resolution, the ANS takes the final step down the hierarchy, collapsing into dorsal vagal shutdown. In this state, the teacher becomes withdrawn, disconnected from students and disinterested in teaching.

Figure 2.3: Example of teacher Polyvagal Theory

Ventral vagal pathway (Relaxed and social)	Ms Smith is engaging with students during a maths lesson until a student with complex needs starts yelling 'school is stupid' and flips his desk.
Sympathetic nervous system (Fight or flight)	Ms Smith has a stress response. She feels anxious and uncertain how to respond to the behaviour. She is hypervigilant and anxious for the next few weeks, anticipating escalated behaviours from the student.
Dorsal vagal pathway (Shutdown)	Ms Smith is not completing lesson preparation or offering extra support to her students. She is withdrawn and feeling hopeless at her job.

Ideally, these three states operate in harmony, allowing you to navigate challenges effectively and return to a sense of safety when threats have passed. However, chronic stress and trauma can impair the brain's ability to accurately assess situations, making it difficult to recognise when an environment is truly safe and disrupting the process of neuroception. This condition, known as 'faulty neuroception', causes your nervous system to misinterpret safe situations as dangerous, leading to heightened anxiety and defensive behaviours even in the absence of real threats. For instance, if you've had a distressing encounter with an aggressive parent, your brain may start perceiving all parents as potential threats. This prolonged activation of self-defence mechanisms can lead to heightened anxiety during parent-teacher interviews and may even result in avoidance behaviours, further reinforcing feelings of stress and unease. Breaking this cycle requires intentional strategies to rebuild a sense of safety and emotional regulation.

Understanding Polyvagal Theory fosters empathy for self and students

By understanding the variability of the different response states, you can better manage your own health and wellbeing and have a better understanding of the behaviour of others. Table 2 outlines the various response states, detailing how you might feel in each and identifying behaviours exhibited by others that signal their emotional state.

Understanding these patterns can be a valuable tool for recognising and responding effectively to student behaviours. By acknowledging that students also experience stress response states, you can view their behaviours through a lens of stress behaviour rather than misbehaviour. For instance, recognising that a student who refuses to complete a test may be feeling anxious and has entered a mobilised state of flight to avoid the perceived threat of the test allows you to approach the situation with empathy rather than frustration. Understanding that the student is reacting, not trying to be disrespectful, gives you the space to respond in a way that acknowledges tests as a trigger for this student and helps you create a plan to support them. Essentially, this trauma-informed response to your student's behaviour helps you stay regulated, preventing the situation from escalating and avoiding heightened emotions for both you and your student.

Table 2: Polyvagal states

	Ventral vagal	Sympathetic nervous system		Dorsal vagal
	Relaxed	Fight	Flight	Shutdown
Looks like	• Calm • Emotionally regulated • Relaxed	• Anger • Irritability • Volatility • Rage	• Panic • Scared • Overwhelm	• Shutdown • Depressed • Hopeless
Feels like	• Grounded and centred • Slow, rhythmic breathing • Mental clarity • Feeling safe	• Tense muscles • Rapid breathing • Sweating	• Nauseous • Difficulty breathing • Shaky	• Feeling numb • Holding breath • Dizzy • Brain fog • Exhaustion
Common actions	• Showing empathy • Connecting with others • Focused and attentive	• Yelling • Swearing • Poor judgement	• Avoidance • Inattention • Rushing (unable to keep still)	• Unable to move • Withdrawing • Lack of motivation

Reflect: Ask yourself the following questions about your nervous system response states:

1. What classroom situations most commonly activate your stress response? (For example, disruptive behaviour, conflict, workload pressure.)
2. When you feel overwhelmed, do you tend to enter a fight or flight (sympathetic) state or a shutdown (dorsal vagal) state?
3. Can you identify specific moments when you feel fully engaged and connected with your students?
4. What are some signs that you are entering a state of alertness or anxiety in the classroom?
5. Have you ever felt disconnected or withdrawn during your teaching? What triggered this response?

Identify what is activating your stress and relaxation responses

Understanding the sensations associated with sympathetic and parasympathetic activation can help you become more aware of what triggers your stress and relaxation responses. For instance, if you notice tightness in your shoulders or chest, take a moment to reflect on what you were just doing or thinking about. Conversely, if you find that your mind feels clear and your breathing is slow, pay attention to your current experience and surroundings.

Polyvagal Theory refers to these moments as triggers (cues that signal a potential threat and activate a fight or flight response) and glimmers (cues that calm your nervous system and make you feel safe). While many of us can pinpoint triggers in our lives, we often overlook the positive impact of recognising glimmers. These small moments of goodness bring us a sense of calm, peace and joy. They help our bodies return to a thriving state and alleviate emotional distress.

Reflect: **Acknowledging that sights, sounds, scents, people or actions can either trigger you or serve as sources of glimmers, take some time to ask yourself the following questions before completing your own list:**

- What makes me feel on edge?
- What makes me feel relaxed?
- What makes me feel withdrawn?

Table 3: Recognising one's personal triggers and glimmers

TRIGGERS	GLIMMERS
• People swearing	• Listening to favourite music
•	•
•	•
•	•
•	•
•	•
•	•

Once you become more aware of your personal triggers and glimmers, you can take conscious action to avoid adverse conditions or intentionally engage in experiences that make you feel safe, calm and connected. For example, if you notice that you always feel grounded and centred when you are in nature, make it a priority to incorporate regular nature experiences into your week.

CHAPTER SUMMARY

- A basic understanding of the autonomic nervous system (ANS) can be empowering and transformative for stress management.
- The ANS has two main components: the sympathetic nervous system (SNS) and parasympathetic nervous system (PNS), which work in balance to regulate involuntary bodily functions.
- The SNS activates the body in response to perceived threats (fight or flight), increasing heart rate, blood pressure and respiration to prepare for action.
- The PNS balances stress hormones and restores calm by promoting relaxation and regulating internal systems, with the vagus nerve playing a key role.
- Polyvagal Theory proposes three adaptive states of the ANS – relaxed (ventral vagal pathway), mobilisation (SNS) and shutdown (dorsal vagal pathway) – each affecting mental health and daily behaviour.
- When functioning harmoniously, neuroception helps you navigate challenges and return to safety after threats. However, chronic stress and trauma can cause 'faulty neuroception', leading to misinterpretation of safe situations as dangerous, resulting in heightened anxiety and defensive behaviours.
- Noticing body sensations, such as tight shoulders (stress trigger) or clear breathing (glimmer), helps improve self-awareness and stress resilience.

CHAPTER 3

I feel exhausted, so why can't I sleep?

The impacts of a dysregulated nervous system

"May you learn to regulate your nervous system to live the life you want instead of staying dysregulated because of the life you have"
– Mastin Kipp

As discussed in the previous chapters, a healthy functioning nervous system is designed to respond to threat by becoming activated and then settling when the threat has decreased. However, when life becomes chaotic and you frequently experience elevated stress, panic or anxiety, an imbalance between your sympathetic nervous system (SNS) and parasympathetic nervous system (PNS) occurs – commonly referred to as nervous system dysregulation.

Figure 3.1: Nervous system imbalance

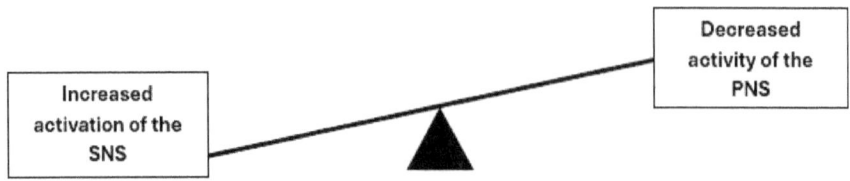

Although dysregulation can occur with an overactive PNS, resulting in lethargy and lack of motivation, it is most common for teachers to experience an imbalance when the SNS is overactive. When this imbalance occurs, the PNS cannot effectively activate to reduce your heart rate, stimulate digestion, facilitate cellular repair or promote relaxation and sleep.

How do I know if my nervous system is dysregulated?

Nervous system imbalance can lead to sustained high cortisol levels, contributing to a myriad of health problems, both physical and emotional. The examples below are not an exhaustive list, but you may find one (or several) that you have experienced or are currently experiencing.

- ☐ You feel tired but find it difficult to unwind
- ☐ You experience restlessness and a continual sense of urgency
- ☐ You feel overwhelmed by daily tasks
- ☐ You have frequent mood swings and irritability
- ☐ You have recurring physical pain or illness
- ☐ You feel anxious or worried, even when things are going well
- ☐ You experience sleep disturbances
- ☐ You overreact and find it difficult to control how you feel
- ☐ You experience panic attacks during stressful situations

In *The Nervous System Reset* (2024), Jessica Maguire suggests that our feelings of anxiety, shutdown, shame, anger or stress are canaries in the coalmine – they're the alarm warning us that we're bumping up against our neurobiological limits. While a deep understanding of neurobiology isn't necessary, it can help explain the emotional and physical responses you're experiencing.

The following table explains the neurobiology of a dysregulated nervous system due to chronic stress.

Table 4: The neurobiology of a dysregulated nervous system

Step	Description
Chronic stress perception	When you experience chronic stress, your brain continuously perceives threats, keeping you in a heightened state of alertness.
Amygdala overactivity	The amygdala, responsible for processing emotions, becomes overactive, constantly signalling the hypothalamus about perceived threats.
Hypothalamus response	The hypothalamus, acting as a command centre, keeps the autonomic nervous system in a prolonged fight or flight state.
Excessive release of stress hormones	The adrenal glands continuously release high levels of cortisol and adrenaline into the bloodstream.
Physical and emotional reactions	Prolonged exposure to stress hormones leads to various physical and emotional reactions, such as increased heart rate, muscle tension, anxiety and difficulty sleeping.
Imbalance in nervous system	The SNS (responsible for fight or flight) remains overactive, while the PNS (responsible for rest and digest) is underactive. This imbalance leads to nervous system dysregulation.

The impacts of too much cortisol in your body

As stated previously, sympathetic overactivation triggers the adrenal glands to release increased amounts of cortisol and adrenaline. While cortisol is necessary in small doses, its continuous release into the bloodstream can interfere with many bodily functions, increasing the likelihood of health issues, as shown in the following figure:

Figure 3.2: Effects of excess cortisol

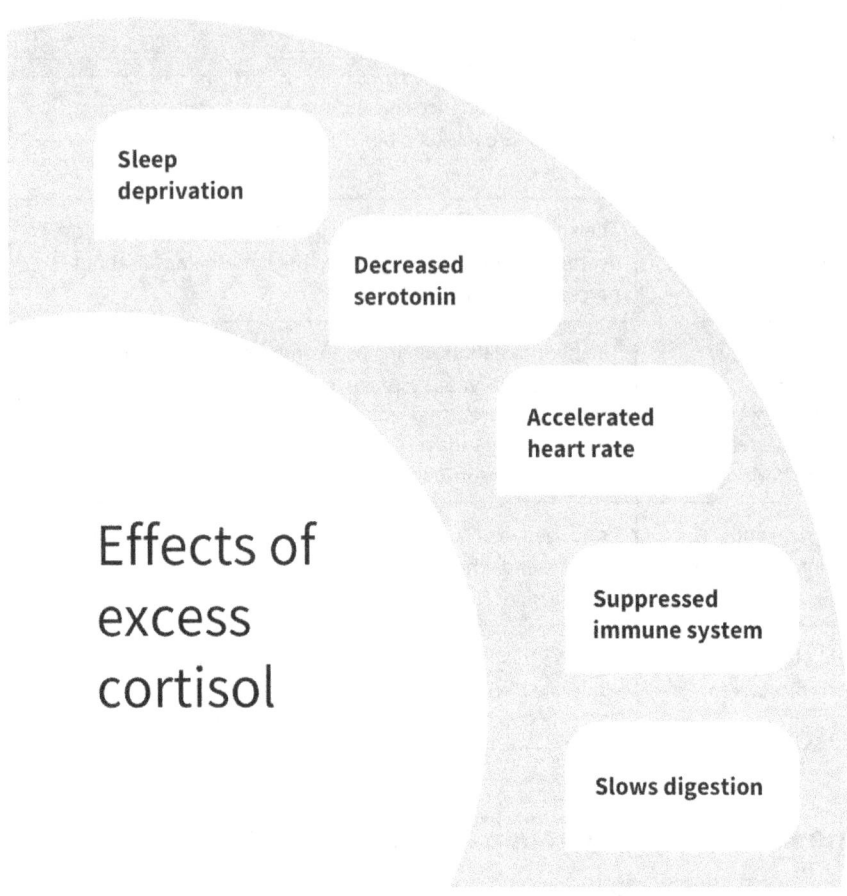

Our body's natural ability to heal is not functioning when our nervous system is dysregulated, therefore, until we can regulate our nervous system, these problems will continue.

Tired but wired

Elevated cortisol levels, caused by an overactive SNS, cause the body to function at a rapid pace. For several years I maintained this pace, believing it to be the most effective way to get everything done. Thankfully, Dr Libby Weaver's book *Rushing Woman's Syndrome* (2017) revealed to me that constant feelings of overwhelm and rush can seriously impact mental and physical wellbeing.

One of the most significant effects is sleep disturbances. When patterns of cortisol production are altered due to overproduction, cortisol levels rise in the evening rather than decline, which can interrupt normal sleep patterns. This experience of being tired but unable to sleep is described by the phrase 'tired but wired'. I recall hearing this expression a few years ago and thinking, 'This is me!' I believed I had insomnia, and despite trying numerous sleep strategies, I continued to experience disturbed sleep for years. Consequently, this negatively impacted my daily functioning and ability to teach.

Relaxation techniques to promote sleep

Emily and Amelia Nagoski, in their book *Burnout: The Secret to Unlocking the Stress Cycle* (2019), emphasise the fundamental role of sleep in overall wellbeing, stating, "Quite simply, we cannot function at our best without it." Although it's common to hear people comparing their lack of sleep as though it is a badge of honour, this is neither healthy nor productive. Sleep is essential for physiological, cognitive, emotional and social functioning. During sleep:

- Your bones, muscles, digestive system and other body tissues restore and repair from any damage
- Your brain processes daily information and forms new memories
- Your body restores energy and releases hormones
- Your immune system strengthens against infections
- Your brain reorganises nerve cells, which supports healthy brain function
- Your muscles relax, including a reduction in heart rate, which consequently lowers your blood pressure

Therefore, prioritising sleep is essential for optimal mental health and wellbeing. I tried many sleep strategies and medicines to help my 'insomnia' because I was unaware that I had all the signs of a dysregulated nervous system. I wasn't listening to my body, and I certainly didn't know that relaxation techniques could activate my PNS, reduce cortisol levels and improve my sleep. Obviously, there may be medical or hormonal reasons for your sleep disturbances, and you should always consult your doctor if you are experiencing sleep deprivation. However, if you think your nervous system is dysregulated and your cortisol levels are high, it might be worth trying these relaxation techniques to activate your relaxation response:

- **Breathing** – Taking slow, deep breaths is one of the easiest ways to trigger your body's natural relaxation response (specific breathing exercises are explained in Chapters 10 and 11).
- **Progressive muscle relaxation** – Tensing and relaxing each muscle group in your body completes the stress response cycle and triggers your relaxation response (progressive muscle relaxation is explained in detail in Chapter 10).
- **Listen to a guided meditation or visualisation** – Our relaxation response will activate when we feel safe. We all know the benefits of reading to children or telling them a story before bedtime. It's comforting! There are many apps which provide stories, guided visualisations or meditations for adults. I personally have used Smiling Mind, Calm and Headspace, but there are many more.

Reflect: Ask yourself the following questions about how stress affects you:

1. How do you typically respond to stressful situations in the classroom? Do you find it hard to calm down afterwards?
2. Have you ever noticed changes in your tone of voice or body language when you feel dysregulated?
3. What coping mechanisms do you instinctively turn to when you are feeling overwhelmed in the classroom?
4. Have you noticed changes in your teaching style or classroom management when you are under significant stress?
5. How does nervous system dysregulation impact your ability to respond to students with patience and empathy?
6. What is your bedtime routine like? Are there any habits that might be impacting your sleep quality?

Isn't it normal to feel this way?

Unfortunately, for many teachers (myself included), constant rushing, fatigue and pain become normal. We become normalised to living in a dysregulated state. In *Rushing Woman's Syndrome* (2017), Dr Libby Weaver uses the following metaphor to explain how we often ignore the symptoms of constant rushing, mental exhaustion, emotional reactivity, frequent illness and poor sleep:

> *If you put a frog in cool water,
> it swims around happily.*
>
> *If you put a frog in boiling water,
> it immediately jumps out to save itself.*
>
> *But if you put a frog into cool water and slowly
> bring that water to the boil, the frog doesn't notice
> and doesn't jump out to save itself.*

When stress steadily continues, we normalise the state of being constantly activated and not experiencing rest. Like the frog in the slow boiling water, we don't notice that our current state is harmful. We dismiss exhaustion with statements like, "Everyone is tired" and we reject feelings of overwhelm by saying, "I am too busy to stop right now." In *The Pruning Principle* (2024), Dr Simon Breakspear and Michael Rosenbrock highlight how feeling overloaded, exhausted and depleted has become the new normal for educators. Over time, teachers have unconsciously rewired their minds to accept this state as inevitable. When visiting schools, Breakspear and Rosenbrock frequently hear educators describe their reality as "just normal, crazy busy", reflecting how deeply embedded this culture of relentless workload has become.

Causes of a maladaptive stress response

In his YouTube series, therapeutic coach Alex Howard (2020) explains that when we consistently operate in a state of dysregulation – where the body remains stuck in fight, flight or freeze mode – we inadvertently reinforce a maladaptive stress response, making it harder to return to a balanced state. A maladaptive stress response refers to an ineffective way of coping with stress, often involving behaviours like avoidance, denial or unhealthy behaviours such as substance abuse. In addition to chronic stress triggering a maladaptive stress response, certain personality traits and exposure to trauma can also contribute to the development of these responses.

Personality trait patterns

Our personality traits can also influence how we cope with stress. We develop patterns of responding to ourselves and others based on these traits. While these patterns aim to protect us and help us cope, they can leave us constantly activated, depleted and exhausted. Howard (2020) defined the following patterns, which, despite having positive qualities, are ultimately unsustainable:

- **Helper pattern** – Seeking validation by constantly doing for others, often at the expense of our own emotional needs.
- **Achiever pattern** – Self-worth is often defined by our actions and achievements in the world. We push ourselves beyond our limits and ignore our body's signals.
- **Perfectionist pattern** – Self-worth is tied to achieving in the right way, with a focus on the correct process. We strive to do the job perfectly, and when we fall short, we feel disappointed or unsafe.
- **Anxiety pattern** – Constantly attempting to think our way to emotional safety, we end up living in our heads rather than being present in our bodies.
- **Controller pattern** – We try to build a sense of safety by controlling ourselves, others and our environment. While this can help us become effective leaders, it often leads to exhaustion because we can never fully control everything and struggle to trust others with delegation.

ACTIVITY 2: Identify your dominant pattern

Read through the following statements to determine your dominant pattern and become more conscious of the beliefs and behaviours which may be leading to a maladaptive stress response:

HELPER
- I often spend most of my time helping others.
- I prioritise other people's needs over my own.
- I feel disconnected from my own needs.
- I derive my sense of self-worth primarily from helping others.

ANXIETY
- I have experienced high levels of anxiety from a young age.
- I have a heightened sense of perceived threats.
- I feel I cannot trust my own inner guidance, opinions and views.
- I constantly worry about what other people think of me.

ACHIEVER
- I hold high expectations for myself and those around me.
- My sense of self-worth is primarily derived from my external achievements.
- One of my greatest fears is being perceived as a failure.
- It is important to me to appear as though I have everything together.

PERFECTIONIST
- I hold high standards for myself and others.
- I constantly strive to get things right.
- I feel like a bad person if I don't achieve perfection.
- My sense of self-worth is primarily derived from doing things the right way.

CONTROLLER
- If I want a job done properly, I need to do it myself.
- The world feels frightening when I'm not in control.
- I'm a natural leader, and in times of crisis, people look to me.
- I'm cautious about sharing my weaknesses and vulnerabilities with others.

Once you become aware of your dominant response patterns – whether rooted in helper tendencies, control-seeking behaviours, achievement-driven perfectionism or anxiety – you can begin making intentional changes to develop more effective coping strategies. By noticing when these patterns arise, you gain the ability to reframe your behaviours in ways that promote healthier, more sustainable responses. For instance, if you identify with the helper pattern, you can begin shifting your perspective – recognising that being supportive does not require self-sacrifice. It's important to remind yourself that others are responsible for their own problems, and intervention isn't always necessary. Instead of thinking, "I must help everyone at all costs," you might reframe your mindset to, "I can support others while maintaining my boundaries."

Making meaningful changes takes time, but self-awareness and intentional adjustments empower you to transform unhelpful response patterns into approaches that nurture both your wellbeing and your relationships. For example, my own journey involved reshaping my anxiety-driven response patterns. Over several years, I gradually replaced anxiety-fuelled behaviours and thought processes by accepting uncertainty and shifting my focus towards mindfulness and presence. While it wasn't a quick fix, consistent reflection helped me recognise how I had broken the cycle of anxious predictions and overthinking, creating space for greater confidence and ease.

CHAPTER SUMMARY

- An overactive SNS often leads to imbalances, making it difficult for the parasympathetic system to activate and restore calm, relaxation and essential functions like sleep and digestion. Signs of dysregulation can include fatigue, restlessness, overwhelm, mood swings, anxiety, sleep disturbances, physical pain and overreactions to stress.
- Chronic stress and elevated cortisol levels disrupt normal bodily functions, leading to issues such as 'tired but wired' sleep patterns, emotional distress and reduced ability to cope.
- Living in a state of constant activation normalises dysregulation, contributing to maladaptive stress responses like denial, avoidance or substance abuse.
- Personality traits like the helper, anxiety, achiever, perfectionist and controller patterns can exacerbate stress by promoting unsustainable behaviours, leaving individuals feeling depleted and exhausted.
- Recognising triggers, understanding your stress patterns and practising relaxation techniques can help improve nervous system balance and restore emotional and physical health.
- Self-awareness and intentional adjustments enable you to transform unhelpful response patterns into nurturing approaches for your wellbeing and relationships.

CHAPTER 4

Why am I so emotional and reactive?

Developing self-awareness to understand your emotions and manage them more effectively

"Neuroscience research shows that the only way we can change the way we feel is by becoming aware of our inner experience and learning to befriend what is going on inside ourselves" – Bessel van der Kolk

We constantly experience emotions, and these emotions influence our mood, behaviours, performance and interactions with others. If your nervous system is dysregulated, it can cause you to respond in disproportionate ways, either overreacting or underreacting. Sadly, emotional reactivity, such as impulsively yelling or crying uncontrollably, is becoming increasingly common among teachers. The popular assumption for why this occurs is that emotions are out of our control, and we are helpless against the things we feel. However, in *Build the Life You Want* (2023), Oprah Winfrey explains that emotions serve as signals to the conscious brain, alerting us to something that requires attention and action. She emphasises that emotions do not define us, nor do they control us – we have the power to decide how to respond to them. Your emotions are messages from your nervous system indicating that something needs to change. If you are not aware of these signals or are repressing negative emotions, emotional reactivity will eventually occur.

Self-awareness is the key to mental health

Through my research and personal application, I've discovered that emotions feel uncontrollable when we lack self-awareness. When was the last time you completely stopped what you were doing, sat in silence for a few minutes and asked yourself, "How am I feeling?" It's not a common practice in teaching, as we are often too busy thinking about how others are feeling.

Reflect: Take a moment to consider how you are feeling right now. Take a deep breath in and then exhale slowly. Close your eyes (if you feel comfortable) and notice the sensations within your body. Ask yourself:

1. How am I feeling?
2. Do you feel any tension or do you feel relaxed?
3. Do you feel at ease or on edge?
4. Does your mind feel cluttered or clear?

As a 'fixer' with a strength in social intelligence, I could always tell how everyone else was feeling, but I wasn't aware of my own emotions. Thankfully, after a few years of practising self-awareness, my life has changed for the better. I am still very conscious of how everyone else is feeling, but now I intentionally make time to check in with my own emotions.

Developing your self-awareness

Self-awareness is a skill that can be developed through intentional practise. By regularly making time to acknowledge your physical sensations, thoughts and feelings, you can develop the ability to:

- Recognise your moment-to-moment emotional experiences
- Handle intense emotions without becoming overwhelmed

Some key strategies to develop self-awareness include:

1. **Observing emotional and physical responses:** The first step to recognising and managing your emotions is to tune in to your body signals, as they are clues to your emotions. In *The Body Keeps the Score* (2014), Bessel van der Kolk explains that becoming aware of your emotions plays a crucial role in fostering emotional regulation. He emphasises that simply acknowledging what you feel helps you stop suppressing or ignoring your internal experiences, allowing for greater emotional balance and healing.
2. **Practising reflection:** The practice that I have found incredibly beneficial for developing self-awareness is journalling. Journalling can be as simple as writing down your thoughts and feelings to understand them more clearly or using journal prompts to assess your thoughts, feelings and behaviours each day. Templates can either be downloaded and printed from the internet, purchased as a premade journal (my favourite is *How are you? A 90-day Check-in Journal* – $14 from Kmart) or you can use an app (I like the free app How We Feel). Look at the journal prompt template below and consider how you would respond to each prompt at this current moment.

Figure 4.1: Journal prompt template

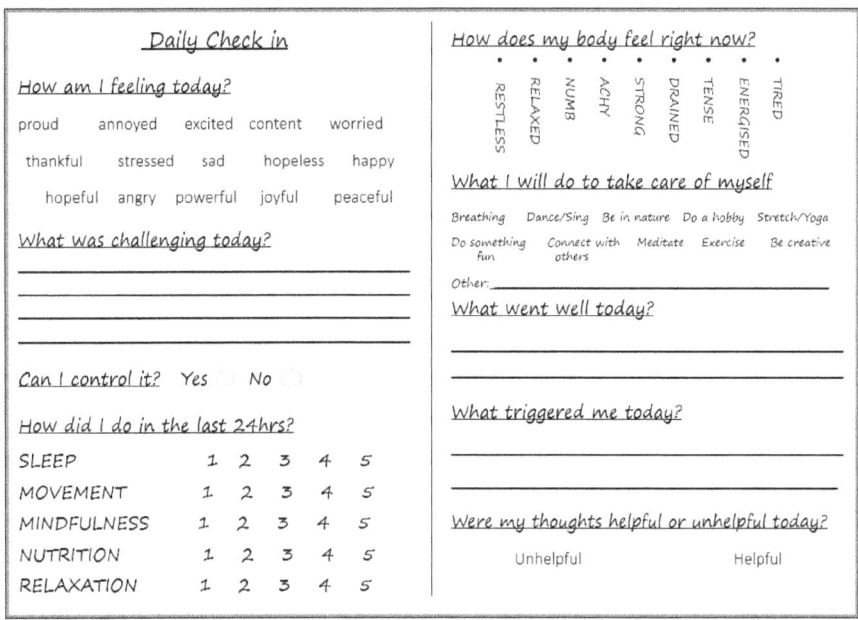

3. **Strengthening emotional intelligence:** Once you become more aware of your physical sensations and feelings, you can identify which emotion you are experiencing and what it is trying to tell you. In *Atlas of the Heart* (2022), Brené Brown highlights that identifying and labelling emotional experiences plays a crucial role in fostering greater emotional regulation and psychological wellbeing. By naming our emotions, we gain a deeper understanding of them, allowing for more effective management and resilience.

   I have listed some emotions commonly recounted by teachers as impacting their daily experiences. Reflecting on Brown's (2022) definitions in *Atlas of the Heart* can deepen your understanding of emotions, offering valuable insights that help clarify and make sense of your own emotional experiences.

   Stress is when we evaluate environmental demand as beyond our ability to cope successfully. This includes elements of unpredictability, uncontrollability and feeling overloaded.

   Overwhelm is an extreme level of stress, an emotional and/or cognitive intensity to the point of feeling unable to function.

   Anxiety is characterised by feelings of tension, worried thoughts and physical changes like increased blood pressure.

   Resentment is the feeling of frustration, judgement, anger, 'better than' and/or hidden envy related to perceived unfairness or injustice. It's an emotion that we often experience when we fail to set boundaries or ask for what we need, or when expectations let us down because they were based on things we can't control, like what other people think, what they feel or how they're going to react.

   Boredom is the uncomfortable state of wanting to engage in satisfying activity but being unable to do it.

   Anger is an emotion that we feel when something gets in the way of a desired outcome or when we believe there is a violation of the way things should be.

4. **Engaging in mindfulness practice:** Meditation, breathwork and present-moment awareness help cultivate deeper emotional insight by allowing you to observe your thoughts and feelings without immediate reaction. By practising mindfulness, you create space between impulse and response, giving yourself the opportunity to pause, reflect and

engage with emotions in a more intentional way. This shift fosters greater emotional regulation, helping you respond thoughtfully rather than reactively in challenging situations.
5. **Observing patterns over time:** Recognising emotional patterns allows you to uncover recurring reactions and gain deeper insight into how you process emotions. By observing the ways you respond to stress, frustration or uncertainty, you can begin identifying underlying emotional themes – such as avoidance, reactivity or self-doubt. Instead of suppressing emotions or letting them dictate your actions, you can learn to acknowledge their presence, notice the physical sensations they create and reflect on what they may be signalling. This awareness helps you break unhelpful cycles, develop healthier emotional responses and create space for greater self-understanding and emotional resilience.

Suppressing and avoiding emotions

Notably, when these emotions arise, they can be distressing and uncomfortable, so sometimes we avoid, dismiss or numb these emotions rather than sit with this discomfort and process the emotion. People use various coping mechanisms – sometimes unconsciously – to avoid experiencing difficult emotions. These avoidance strategies can provide temporary relief but may lead to long-term emotional distress if used excessively. Some common ways people avoid uncomfortable emotions include:

- Keeping excessively busy to avoid sitting with emotions
- Binge-watching TV or scrolling social media, to numb difficult feelings
- Saying, "I'm fine" or "it's not a big deal" even when feeling overwhelmed
- Using substances like alcohol, food or drugs to numb emotional pain
- Avoiding conflict or difficult conversations to prevent feeling vulnerable
- Saying "yes" to requests even when overwhelmed, to avoid confronting stress or anxiety
- Minimising emotions by saying, "it's not that bad" or "others have it worse"

Your beliefs affect your ability to process emotions

Ignoring or suppressing emotions means that we are not acknowledging what our nervous system is trying to tell us. This can occur because we have been conditioned to believe certain things about emotions.

Reflect: Ask yourself the following questions about your emotional beliefs:

1. How did you learn to recognise, understand and express your emotions?
2. Were you ever taught how to express emotions in a healthy manner?
3. Were there certain emotions you were discouraged from feeling or expressing as a child?

In *Toxic Positivity* (2022), Whitney Goodman highlights that our ability to express and regulate emotions is shaped by life experiences, particularly during childhood. She emphasises that if emotional expression feels challenging, it's important to remember that learning to feel and articulate emotions is a skill – one we may not have been taught effectively. It is not the fault of our parents and caregivers. My mum was wonderful at teaching me to understand emotions and express my feelings. However, without realising it, she frequently attempted to reframe all my emotions in a positive light – encouraging me to "be grateful", "look on the bright side" and "put on a happy face". So I did, becoming a cheerful, nurturing teacher who focused solely on the positives while disregarding any negative or uncomfortable feelings – until they inevitably built up and overflowed.

Over the past few years, I have observed the following conditioned beliefs in other teachers. Review this list, noting if any of the statements resonate with you:

- Negative emotions are bad and should be avoided.
- I will appear 'ungrateful' or 'negative' if I demonstrate negative emotions.
- Being emotional is a sign of vulnerability, and vulnerability is weakness.
- I should be happy most or all of the time.
- If I tell other people how I feel, they will think I can't cope with my job.

Conditioned beliefs about emotions can shape how you react in moments of stress or overwhelm. If you routinely repress uncomfortable emotions – such as anxiety, stress or resentment – they can build up over time, eventually leading to intense emotional turmoil. This might manifest as uncontrollable crying, shutting down, explosive anger or the urge to escape. Becoming aware of these underlying beliefs allows you to shift your emotional responses. Rather than instinctively avoiding discomfort, you can learn to sit with the physical sensations of an emotion, creating space to uncover its deeper message. Every emotion carries valuable insight – whether it signals an unmet need, a boundary being crossed or unresolved experiences seeking acknowledgement. By engaging with your emotions instead of suppressing them, you foster a healthier relationship with yourself – one grounded in emotional awareness, acceptance and resilience.

Develop interoception and learn to feel the physical sensations

Avoiding emotions can also be linked to poor interoceptive awareness. Interoception is the perception of internal sensations and is often referred to as the eighth sense because it gathers information about how your body parts feel. Your brain uses the information about the way your body feels as clues to your current emotion(s): are you hungry, nervous, tired, sick, excited? Thus, interoception awareness is necessary to notice when you are becoming angry, anxious, collapsed or shut down so that you can manage your emotions proactively rather than reactively. In *The Vagus Nerve Reset* (2023), Anna Ferguson emphasises that understanding and acknowledging our emotions – both what we feel and why we feel it – enhances our ability to regulate them effectively, ultimately empowering us to take control of our emotional wellbeing and our lives.

Although our thoughts provide some insight into our emotional state, it is the inner signals that supply the majority of information to the brain, helping determine whether we are safe or in danger. For example, if your heart is racing, your interoceptive awareness will urge you to seek comfort from others or do something to change your current situation, which makes you feel safe and calm. Therefore, your interoceptive body sensations are key in motivating you to self-regulate and take actions that restore comfort within your body.

Interoception awareness is particularly important if you find yourself regularly pushed out of your window of tolerance into hypo-arousal. When this occurs, people often become disassociated from their body, in a shutdown state. Developing or improving interoception awareness is vital in this situation, as you need to engage in up-regulating strategies which help you reconnect with your body and notice signals early to help you move back into your window of tolerance.

Daily practices to develop interoception

To develop interoceptive awareness, you can practise mindfulness techniques like body scans, breathing techniques and somatic movements. To ensure you find time to practise these techniques and experience their optimal benefits, I suggest integrating mindfulness practice into your daily routine. Fortunately, studies have shown that practising these techniques with your students not only enhances your wellbeing but also improves the wellbeing of your students. Brunzell et al. (2021) suggest that when teachers practise the same wellbeing strategies they want their students to practise, teachers feel more connected and resilient in their work. For example, if we want our students to breathe from their belly, teachers must model and make that strategy into an everyday routine. If teachers want students to take rhythmic brain breaks to develop stamina and persistence for learning, teachers also benefit when they participate in these same brain breaks. Student wellbeing and teacher wellbeing are delicately reciprocating, so we want to show them by example that wellbeing strategies when learning are worth our collective efforts. In Chapter 11, you will find examples of mindfulness techniques and ideas for practising them with your students.

Reflect: Ask yourself the following questions to encourage self-reflection and emotional awareness:

1. How do you typically recognise and process your emotions throughout the school day?
2. Are there moments when you suppress emotions rather than acknowledge them? Why?
3. Are you able to recognise when your nervous system needs regulation? If so, what signs do you notice?

4. Do you use interoceptive awareness (tuning in to bodily sensations) to help manage stress?
5. How do you reset or restore balance when your body signals emotional or physical discomfort?

CHAPTER SUMMARY

- Emotions are signals from the nervous system that require attention and action. Lack of awareness or suppression can lead to emotional reactivity.
- Developing self-awareness helps manage emotions, prevent overwhelm and foster mental health by recognising physical sensations, thoughts and feelings.
- Strategies to develop self-awareness include observing emotional and physical responses, practising reflection, strengthening emotional intelligence, engaging in mindfulness practice and observing patterns over time.
- Interoception is the perception of internal body sensations, providing clues to emotional states, enabling proactive self-regulation and fostering emotional control.
- Suppressing emotions or adhering to conditioned beliefs about emotions can result in heightened emotional turmoil, leading to reactivity such as impulsive outbursts or shutdowns.
- Techniques such as body scans, breathing exercises and somatic movements enhance interoceptive awareness, helping maintain emotional balance and resilience.
- Teachers modelling mindfulness strategies for students not only improve personal wellbeing but also strengthen their connection and resilience in the classroom.

PART 2
SELF-EMPOWERMENT

TECHNIQUES AND STRATEGIES FOR REDUCING AND MANAGING STRESS

CHAPTER 5

How can I avoid taking work-related stress home with me?

The importance of completing the stress response cycle

"90% of what you're stressing about right now won't even matter a year from now. Take a deep breath" – Mel Robbins

Work-life balance is an elusive concept for most educators, likely because our autonomic nervous system does not distinguish between work and home environments. While the stressors may not follow you home, the stress retained in your body does. In an episode of the *Trauma Informed Educators Network* podcast (2023), Mathew Portell referred to this as "all-life balance". He explained that our nervous systems are constantly active in all areas of life, so if your nervous system is in survival mode at work, it will often default to survival mode at home. This truly resonated with me, reminding me of the times I came home from work feeling stressed and overreacted to everyday tasks like taking my children to sports practice or cooking dinner.

In the book *Burnout: The Secret to Unlocking the Stress Cycle* (2019), Emily and Amelia Nagoski emphasise the importance of dealing with workplace stress so that it is not stored in the body:

> *"The good news is that stress is not the problem. It's how we deal with stress – not what causes it – that releases the stress, completes the cycle, and ultimately, keeps us from burning out. You can't control every external stressor that comes your way. The goal isn't to live in a state of perpetual balance and peace and calm; the goal is to move through stress to calm, so that you're ready for the next stressor, and to move from effort to rest and back again."*

Many of the stressors depicted in Figure 5.1 are out of your control. Increased workload is undoubtedly one of the biggest stressors for teachers. However, like many stressors within the education system, it is not something that individual teachers can control.

Figure 5.1: Teacher stressors

The difference between stressors and stress

To effectively manage stress, it's crucial to understand the difference between stressors and stress. Stressors are events or environments that you might find demanding, challenging or threatening to your safety. Stress, on the other hand, is the neurological and physiological shift that occurs in your body when you encounter one of these threats. Studies in positive psychology suggest that it is not the potential stressor itself, but how you perceive and handle it that determines whether it will lead to stress.

It is important to acknowledge that many stressors are beyond your control. However, knowing what triggers your stress is essential, as it allows you to develop coping strategies for specific situations and activities. Furthermore, understanding your stressors can help you manage your emotional responses more effectively and increase the likelihood of noticing signs of stress in your body when you encounter those stressors. By completing the following activity, you can identify which work-related stressors cause you the most stress.

ACTIVITY 3: Identify which stressors cause you work-related stressed

Self-evaluation of stressors

On a scale of 1 to 5, how much do the following situations cause you stress?

Place an X on the number that best represents your experience.

Not at all stressed		Moderately stressed		Extremely stressed
1	2	3	4	5

Administration demands/workload

1   2   3   4   5

Engaging in parent interactions/meeting parent expectations

1   2   3   4   5

Teaching students with complex learning, social and behavioural needs

1   2   3   4   5

Lack of resources/professional development to teach effectively

1   2   3   4   5

Emotionally supporting students with challenging/traumatic backgrounds

1   2   3   4   5

Managing challenging/violent student behaviours

1   2   3   4   5

Having to take on extra responsibilities/duties/class supervisions

1   2   3   4   5

Why stress becomes stuck in your body

Understanding your personal stressors is helpful; however, sometimes even when the stressors are gone, stress remains in the body. This is because if we ignore or suppress the stress response, the energy becomes stuck in our bodies.

So, why might we ignore or suppress stress?

People overlook or suppress stress for various reasons. However, for educators, two specific reasons come to mind:

1. The high demands of managing challenging student behaviours
2. Societal expectations to consistently display composure

When you have a student with complex needs or challenging behaviours in your class for a term, semester or year, you know that you must face that stressor repeatedly. Consequently, your stress response may become permanently activated, making stress feel normal and often overlooked. Unlike most people, when a teacher's stress response is activated, we often suppress it because our reaction is not socially appropriate. We can't scream or swear at a child when we feel angry; we can't run out of the room when presenting to colleagues (even though we feel terrified); and we can't tell a parent that their child is a spoiled brat!

In these situations, we are flooded with adrenaline and cortisol, priming us to 'survive'. However, because we don't react with a fight or flight response and move the energy, we become soaked in stress hormones. Consequently, if this occurs regularly, our cortisol levels remain extremely high, which, as stated in Chapter 3, can have several detrimental effects on our physical, mental and emotional wellbeing. This is why completing the stress cycle is beneficial for your wellbeing.

Completing the stress cycle

Simply put, completing the stress cycle is the moment when our bodies recognise that we have faced danger and are now safe. It is the completion of the full cycle of stress: identification, activation, mobilisation and relaxation. The stress response is an evolutionary adaptive process designed to keep us safe, and like many biological processes, it has a beginning, middle and end. A perceived threat activates neurological and hormonal responses that initiate physiological changes to mobilise your body for survival. This cycle, often related to survival, is depicted in Figure 5.2.

Figure 5.2: Stress in prehistoric times

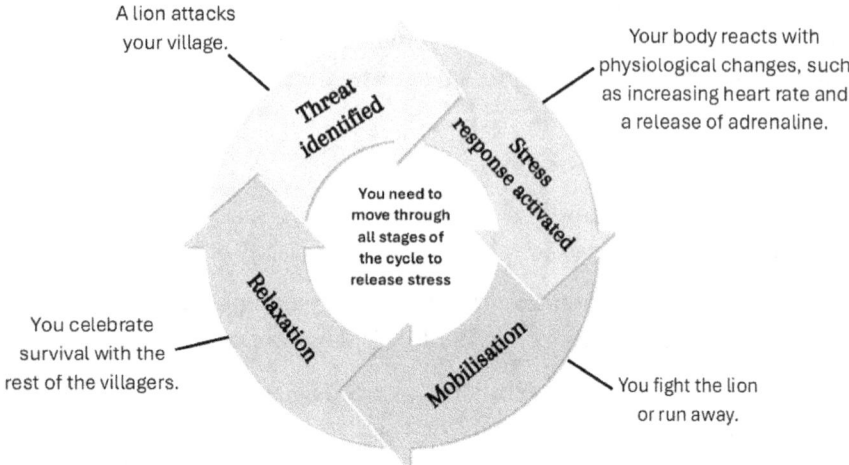

In prehistoric times the stress response helped humans survive the very real threat of predators, however, in modern-day society the stress response is often activated by psychological rather than physical threats, as seen in Figure 5.3.

Figure 5.3: Stress in modern-day society (for a teacher)

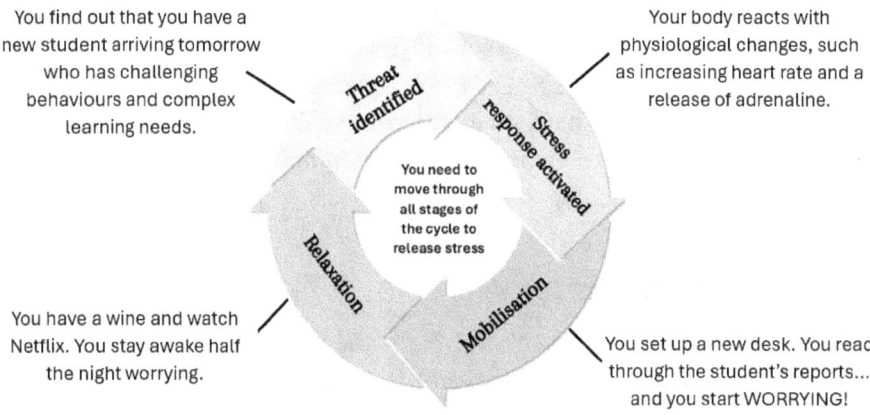

In this example, physical mobilisation and relaxation have not been achieved, so the stress hormones activated during the stress response have not been released and are still circulating through the body. The stress remains stored because the teacher's body is still in the middle of the stress cycle. Unlike the prehistoric example, the teacher does not need to move to survive, but her nervous system does not know that. It has perceived a psychological threat and is priming her body for survival – to fight, flee or freeze. To complete the stress response cycle, her body needs a signal that it is safe.

How to complete the stress cycle

In *Burnout: The Secret to Unlocking the Stress Cycle* (2019), Emily and Amelia Nagoski emphasise that engaging in physical activity is the most effective way to complete the stress response cycle, allowing the body to process and release accumulated tension. This is because moving your body mobilises the energy which has been created by adrenaline, and this tells your brain that you have survived a threat and are now safe.

But don't worry if you hate the gym. There are numerous ways to move your body that don't require sweating profusely. Figure 5.4 includes some other evidence-based ways to complete the stress cycle.

Figure 5.4: Ways to complete the stress response cycle

1. **Move your body.** Any physical activity which makes your muscles move and pump blood through your body will reduce adrenaline and stress hormones created during the stress response. Virtually any form of movement, from running to yoga, will release stress. Even tensing and releasing your muscles or stretching a resistance band will signal to your body that it is safe.
2. **Have a cry.** How often have you found yourself crying and you don't know why? Sometimes our body knows that we have stress built up and it needs to be released through crying. Unfortunately, we often suppress our tears and apologise for crying, but we shouldn't because the physiological act of crying is our body's way of releasing the stress hormones accumulated from the stress response.
3. **Breathe.** Short, shallow breaths signal to your body and brain that you are unsafe, but by intentionally controlling your breath to become slower and longer, you communicate a sense of safety through your body. Deep, slow breaths with a long exhalation downregulate the stress response and promote a sense of calmness. There are numerous breathing techniques you can use, but it is important to find the ones which work best for you. Personally, I find box breathing very easy and effective, but in Chapters 9, 10 and 11 you will also be introduced to a variety of other breathing techniques.
4. **Connection and physical affection.** Connection with others (especially trusted friends and family) helps us feel safer because we know that others are looking out for us. Even if you can't meet in person, calling or FaceTiming allows you to experience connection. If you don't want to communicate verbally, you can still connect with others through physical affection. Expressing and receiving affection through physical touch helps your body to release trust and bonding hormones like oxytocin. For example, hugging a trusted person (or even a pet) for 20 seconds lowers your heart rate and communicates to your body that you are safe.
5. **Go to your safe space.** Experiencing 'felt safety' will activate the relaxation response and this can occur when you 'go to your safe space'. However, it is important to note that feeling safe is different to being safe. Sometimes we are physically safe, but we do not feel it. This is why your safe space may not be a physical space but rather a song, blanket, scent, person, pet, memory, object or visualisation. Ultimately, it is whatever makes you truly feel safe.

Completing the stress response cycle at work

Understanding the stress response cycle and how to complete it is crucial for all teachers to prevent the build-up of unprocessed stress. By choosing one of the ways to complete the stress response cycle throughout the day, before you go home or as soon as you get home, you can essentially avoid taking work stress home with you. Part 3 of this book provides numerous examples of practices that can be embedded into your workday to ensure you are completing the stress response cycle.

Although stressors will persist throughout the year, you will be taking intentional action to reduce stress and prevent emotional exhaustion and burnout. This is illustrated in Figure 5.5, where the teacher completes the stress response cycle by doing a progressive muscle relaxation activity to move the energy. This cue tells her body that the threat is gone and allows her to connect and relax back to a neutral state.

Figure 5.5: Completing the stress response cycle effectively

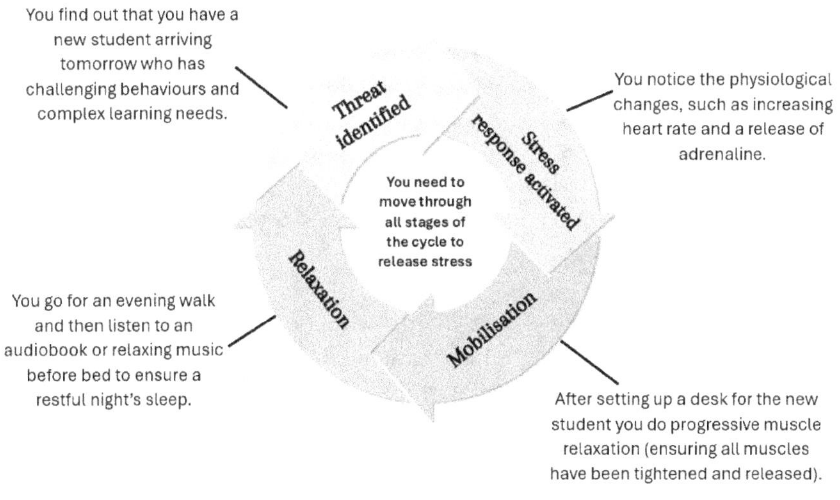

- You find out that you have a new student arriving tomorrow who has challenging behaviours and complex learning needs. **(Threat identified)**
- You notice the physiological changes, such as increasing heart rate and a release of adrenaline. **(Stress response activated)**
- After setting up a desk for the new student you do progressive muscle relaxation (ensuring all muscles have been tightened and released). **(Mobilisation)**
- You go for an evening walk and then listen to an audiobook or relaxing music before bed to ensure a restful night's sleep. **(Relaxation)**

You need to move through all stages of the cycle to release stress

Although the stressor of a new student will still be there tomorrow, the teacher was able to take simple actions to complete the stress response cycle, which allowed her to have a restful night's sleep and approach the situation in a calm, logical state – not in survival mode.

Reflect: Ask yourself the following questions:

1. What activities or practices help you feel calm and relaxed after a stressful day?
2. Have you tried physical activities like exercise or deep breathing to help complete the stress response cycle?
3. How do you process and release emotions related to stress? Do you talk to someone, journal or use other methods?
4. How effective are your current strategies for managing and completing the stress response cycle?
5. What changes or improvements can you make to your stress management practices?

CHAPTER SUMMARY

- While many stressors are beyond your control, knowing your triggers is essential for developing coping strategies and managing emotional responses.
- Understanding your stressors helps you notice signs of stress in your body and better handle work-related challenges.
- Stress is a physiological response to perceived threats, and managing the stress response cycle – from activation to relaxation – is crucial to prevent burnout.
- Ignoring or suppressing stress, often due to professional demands or societal expectations, leads to accumulated stress hormones, causing physical, mental and emotional strain.
- Physical activity is the most effective way to complete the stress response cycle, signalling safety to the body and releasing built-up stress hormones.
- Additional strategies for stress relief, including crying, controlled breathing, connection with others and experiencing 'felt safety', can help reduce stress and restore balance in the body.
- Teachers benefit from understanding and completing the stress response cycle to avoid bringing work stress home, ensuring better overall wellbeing.

CHAPTER 6

How can I reduce stress when I never have enough time?

How to manage your energy rather than your time

"Yesterday I was clever, so I wanted to change the world. Today I am wise, so I am changing myself" – Rumi

Many of the wellbeing initiatives promoted by education departments focus on improving teachers' nutrition, sleep and exercise routines. Although these initiatives are well-intentioned, I have heard many teachers questioning how they can fit more in, given their already limited time. This is because time is finite, so we never feel like we have enough of it. In contrast, our energy can be regularly renewed. By intentionally scheduling specific routines into your day, you can actually boost your energy levels, better manage stress and enhance your overall wellbeing.

"Energy is transferable and absorbable"

The Collins Dictionary defines energy as "the ability and strength to do active physical things and the feeling that you are full of physical power and life". In her book *Energy: Get it. Guard it. Give it.* (2024), Lisa O'Neill extends on this definition by stating that "Energy is the essence of our existence. We are all energetic beings, and understanding the dynamics of energy is the key to unlocking our true potential. Our energy is transferable and absorbable." O'Neill's explanation of energy being 'transferable and absorbable' is especially pertinent to teachers. Every day you are engaging in hundreds of interactions – answering questions, giving instructions, planning with colleagues and conversing with parents. The countless decisions, interactions and conversations that fill a typical day can drain the mental and emotional energy of even the most energetic teachers. Additionally, a high level of physical energy is required to get though a day of teaching. Most teachers stand up throughout their lesson delivery, coach sporting teams and walk around during playground duty. And let's not forget early childhood teachers, who engage with energetic little people all day and rarely sit down! Thankfully, our energy is not limited, so regardless of how much we give, we can make intentional choices to protect and replenish it.

Embracing energy as your life force

I think of energy as my life force. After 15 years of practising yoga, I have come to understand the flow of energy and respect the power it brings to various aspects of my life. Energy comes from four main sources in human beings: the body, emotions, mind and spirit, and each of these four dimensions needs to be managed for optimal wellbeing.

Physical energy is associated with the energy of our body. We all know how great it feels when our body is energised with good nutrition, enough sleep and regular exercise, and we all know how rotten our body feels when we have eaten too much sugar, haven't slept well and haven't engaged in any physical movement for weeks. Whether we want to admit it or not, our lifestyle decisions affect the energy we have in our bodies. When you are feeling tired, the last thing you feel like doing is exercise, however, exercise actually changes your body physically to help you feel more energetic. Engaging in physical activity increases blood flow, boosts oxygen circulation and releases endorphins – the feel-good hormones.

Emotional energy comes from how we feel and is driven by our emotions. Due to the relational nature of teaching, the emotional energy reservoir of a teacher runs down quicker than most professions. This is because the foundation of successful teaching is based on ongoing, emotional interactions with students. You are simultaneously putting emotional investment into your students' wellbeing and academic success, absorbing their emotions and trying to manage your own. In response to these conflicting priorities, many teachers dismiss their own emotions to direct their emotional energy into supporting their students. This imbalance is not helpful as it ultimately drains your emotional energy and leaves you with nothing left to give to yourself, your students or your family.

Mental energy originates in the mind and refers to our ability to think and perform cognitive tasks. Teachers are experts at thinking and performing cognitive tasks – it comes with the job description. Unfortunately, it does not mean that we have limitless mental energy. In fact, due to the intellectual demands and requirement to consistently be making decisions, mental energy can quickly become depleted for teachers. Recently, a colleague mentioned that after a short period of leave, she needed an afternoon sleep after her first day back at work. She acknowledged that she was mentally exhausted after only one day back in the classroom, and that she couldn't even think of what to cook for dinner or have a chat with her husband because she was so mentally drained. Can you relate?

Every day you are constantly planning, assessing, questioning, solving problems, multitasking, evaluating, making adjustments, observing, responding to behaviours… the mental list is endless and often leads to overthinking. Subsequently, one of the best ways to boost mental energy is to determine what you can and can't control and set boundaries. In fact, this is such an important element of self-preservation that Chapter 7 is dedicated to letting go of things you can't control and setting boundaries.

Spiritual energy comes from your internal spirit – your inner self. Spirituality is not about religion. It is about being connected to something greater than yourself. It is about your purpose, your intentions and your meaningful connections. Spiritually energised people are less inclined to experience work-related tasks as stressful because they identify meaning in their work. I believe many of you will agree that teaching provides a meaningful purpose in life, which can enhance your spiritual energy. However, if you experience high anxiety or feel disconnected, it might be necessary to focus on connecting with your inner self and finding meaning and purpose away from your role as a teacher.

Reflect: Ask yourself the following questions:

1. What physical symptoms do you notice when you are low on energy, and how do you address them?
2. What are your eating habits like? Do you feel your diet supports your energy levels throughout the day?
3. How do you manage your workload to prevent mental fatigue and burnout?
4. Do you have any spiritual practices or rituals that help you feel grounded and energised? What are they?
5. What goals can you set to better manage your physical, emotional, mental and spiritual energy?

Recognising energy-depleting behaviours

When we are not intentional about managing our energy, it is easy to fall into habits which deplete energy. By completing the activity opposite, you may identify some behaviours which could be depleting your energy. By becoming aware of these behaviours, you can make intentional choices to change your actions and safeguard your energy.

ACTIVITY 4: Self-assessment of energy-depleting behaviours

	Behaviour	Like me	Unlike me
Physical	Not drinking enough water		
	Not having a lunchbreak every day		
	Limited regular movement/exercise		
	Eating sugary snacks/drinking caffeine when you feel tired		
Emotional	Using negative self-talk		
	Complaining about work/gossiping		
	'People pleasing' by taking on too many responsibilities		
	Continually worrying or catastrophising		
Mental	Frequently multitasking		
	Working nonstop without a break		
	Not expressing your needs and boundaries to colleagues		
	Overthinking lesson plans		
Spiritual	Avoiding real connections and choosing to scroll on social media		
	Not making time to do things which bring you joy		
	Valuing others above yourself		
	Not connecting with yourself through prayer/journalling/meditation		

Take responsibility for replenishing your energy

Certain thoughts, behaviours and interactions can drain your energy. When you become aware of diminishing energy, you can choose to replenish it. Many of us overlook the signs of dwindling energy and continue working instead of addressing the needs of our body and mind. Well-meaning individuals might suggest that you "get a good night's sleep" or "take a rest" to combat low energy. However, you may not see any improvement until you approach managing low energy holistically.

Table 5 indicates the signs of diminishing energy and immediate actions you can take to replenish each energy source. This can be as simple as pausing your lesson when you notice yourself repeatedly yawning and taking a three-minute break to drink some water or walk outside with your students. Most educators know the benefits of brain breaks to increase student engagement and productivity, but it is imperative to remember that these breaks are just as important for teachers to manage their energetic needs throughout the day.

Table 5: Signs of diminishing energy

ENERGY	SIGNS OF DIMINISHING ENERGY	INSTANT ENERGISING ACTION
Physical	Yawning Hunger Restlessness Sleepiness	• Drink water
Emotional	Withdrawing from others Irritability Numbness Low sensory tolerance	• Laugh – watch or listen to something funny
Mental	Difficulty concentrating Lack of motivation Difficulty making decisions	• Move your body – stretch, stand up or walk around
Spiritual	Boredom Anxiety Feeling disconnected	• Engage in the 5-4-3-2-1 grounding technique (details found in Chapter 12)

Routines to boost and preserve your energy

After identifying which sources of your energy are most depleted, you can intentionally boost and preserve your energy throughout the day. As a teacher, your day is full of routines designed to create safe, predictable environments for students, reducing cognitive load and unnecessary stress. Creating routines for yourself is just as necessary. Managing your energy is something you control, and you can take intentional action to become more energised.

Table 6 shows routines that can be embedded into your day to boost and preserve energy levels. To see an increase in your most depleted energy source, start by choosing one or two practices from that source area and incorporating them into your day.

Table 6: Daily routines to boost and preserve energy levels

PHYSICAL	EMOTIONAL
• Get your body moving (for example, dancing, stretching, walking, yoga, swimming) • Spend time in the sun • Meal plan to ensure you are eating nutritious meals • Drink water regularly throughout the day (use a visual reminder or timer) • Stop to eat lunch (preferably away from your desk) • Make time to go to the bathroom • Go to bed at a similar time each night and reduce screen time before bed	• Prioritise time to do things you enjoy (write these activities on your work and home calendars) • Make time for fun with your students (tell jokes, watch a funny video or join in games) • Get inspired (read or listen to stories of inspirational people) • Plan something to look forward to (an evening with friends or a holiday) • Surround yourself with things that make you feel happy (display photos, play your favourite music or hang brightly coloured curtains)

MENTAL	SPIRITUAL
• Only reply to emails at designated times (for example, before school, after school, not after 5pm) • Take work emails off your phone • Use AI technologies to reduce workload • Reduce multitasking (completing one task at a time is more effective and less taxing on mental load) • Write daily to-do lists and cross them off • During non-contact/release time put a note on your door saying 'DO NOT DISTURB (unless it's an emergency)' or find another space to work	• Journal in the morning or at night (writing in a journal helps to connect with your inner self) • Make time to be in nature (ground yourself by walking barefoot on the grass or teach your lesson outdoors) • Make time for silence (sit quietly in your car for three minutes before you drive home) • Be in the present moment (name 5 things you can see, 4 things you can feel, 3 things you can hear, 2 things you can smell and 1 thing you can taste)

CHAPTER SUMMARY

- While time is limited, energy can be renewed through intentional routines that enhance stress management and overall wellbeing.
- Energy is the essence of existence; it is transferable and absorbable, and managing it is key to unlocking potential.
- Human energy arises from the body, emotions, mind and spirit – all of which require proactive management for optimal balance.
- Exercise, good nutrition and adequate sleep boost physical energy by increasing blood flow, oxygen circulation and releasing endorphins.
- Teachers often deplete emotional energy due to constant interactions, absorbing student emotions while neglecting their own needs.
- The cognitive demands of teaching can exhaust mental energy; setting boundaries and prioritising tasks can help restore it.
- Connecting with purpose, meaningful relationships and inner self can enhance resilience, reduce stress and replenish energy.

CHAPTER 7

How can I find time for myself when there is so much on my to-do-list?

Letting go of things you can't control and setting boundaries

"We need to do better at putting ourselves higher on our own 'to-do' list" – Michelle Obama

Teachers face numerous stressors, including parental demands, increased workloads and a lack of resources. Managing these stressors in the high-intensity, fast-paced environment of a school can make it feel like there's never a moment to stop and rest. I believe the following parable from Stephen Covey's *The 7 Habits of Highly Effective People* (2020) effectively illustrates this concept, offering valuable insight into its practical application.

Suppose you came upon a man in the woods working feverishly to saw down a tree. "What are you doing?" you ask.

"Can't you see?" comes the impatient reply. "I'm sawing down a tree."

You exclaim: "You look exhausted! How long have you been at it?"

> *The man replies: "Over five hours, and I'm beat! This is hard work."*
>
> *You inquire: "Well, why don't you take a break for a few minutes and sharpen your saw? I'm sure it will go a lot faster."*
>
> *The man emphatically replies: "I don't have time to sharpen the saw. I'm too busy sawing."*

This is the paradox of teaching. Just like the man in the parable, most teachers feel stressed, but they are too busy teaching to stop and recharge their tank. Undoubtedly, the process of teaching demands a high level of mental, emotional and physical energy, leaving little capacity to deal with other stressors such as parental demands, administrative tasks and increased accountability.

So, how can you find time to reduce stress? The key is to take control – not of the stressors, but of the one thing you can control: yourself. It's not about eliminating stressors but about building resilience and responding to them in a balanced way. By taking proactive steps, you can create a more peaceful and manageable life.

Many aspects of education are beyond your control, but you can manage your energy, time, reactions and behaviours. In *Wellbeing Leadership: A New Approach for School Leaders* (2024), Amy Green argues that instead of school leaders attempting to fix or rescue overwhelmed teachers – a pattern seen historically – it is far more empowering to use coaching questions. This approach helps teachers to reflect on their challenges, identify their own solutions and take meaningful action towards change.

Thrive within your sphere of control

The lack of adequate resources, constant policy changes and unachievable administrative tasks impact your day as a teacher – but you cannot control them. In *The 7 Habits of Highly Effective People* (2020), Covey explains that individuals can either be proactive or reactive. Proactive people direct their energy towards actions within their control, focusing on what they can influence. In contrast, reactive individuals tend to fixate on external factors beyond their control, often adopting a mindset of victimisation and blame. Covey emphasises that developing a proactive approach leads to greater personal effectiveness and resilience. He conceptualised this into a model widely referred to as the 'circles of control'.

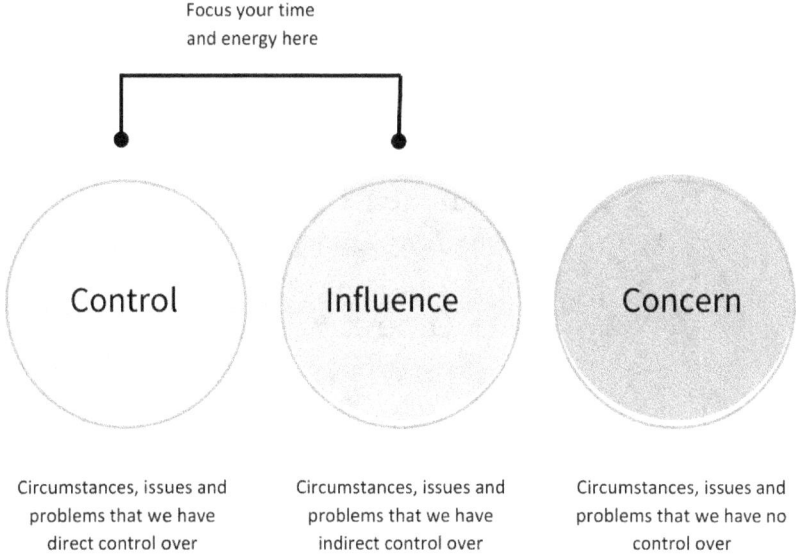

Figure 7.1: Circles of control

In *Thriving Together* (2025), David Kolpak emphasises that recognising the distinction between what you can influence and what lies beyond your control is crucial for safeguarding your wellbeing, especially in a school environment where external factors – such as institutional policies, strategic decisions and students' home situations – remain outside your direct influence. By focusing on what is within your sphere of control, you can cultivate a healthier, more resilient approach to challenges rather than expending valuable time and emotional resources on aspects that cannot be changed. This principle is effectively illustrated in Figure 7.1

As educators, there are many problems or issues that may concern you, and it is easy to become overwhelmed by these. For example, you may be concerned about a student's behaviour and the lack of parental support. However, the only thing you can control is your reaction towards the student. Worrying or complaining about the child's lack of parenting will not change their experience, but you can enhance their experience at school by showing that you care and accept them. The example in Figure 7.2 demonstrates how the circles of control can be a valuable tool for classifying your challenges as a teacher and effectively distributing your limited time and energy to address them.

Figure 7.2: Circles of control – teacher example

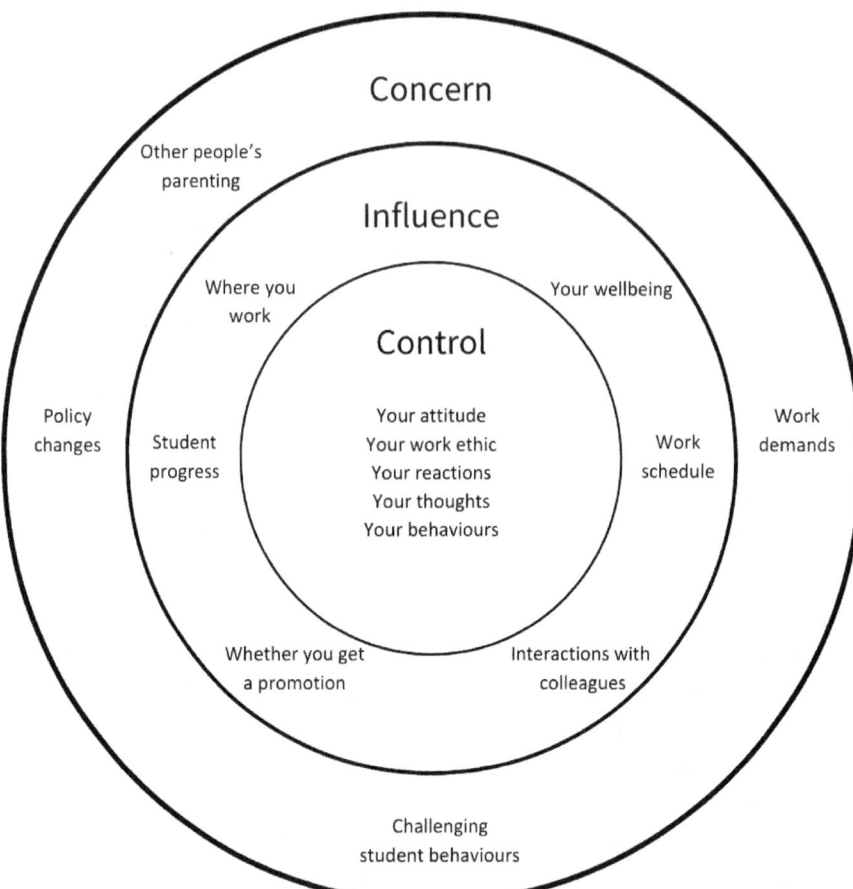

ACTIVITY 5: Your circles of control

Now it's time for you to think about your circles of control.

1. In the outer ring, list those things that you are concerned about but can't control or influence.
2. In the inner circle, list those things you are concerned about and can influence.
3. In the centre, list those things you have control over right now.

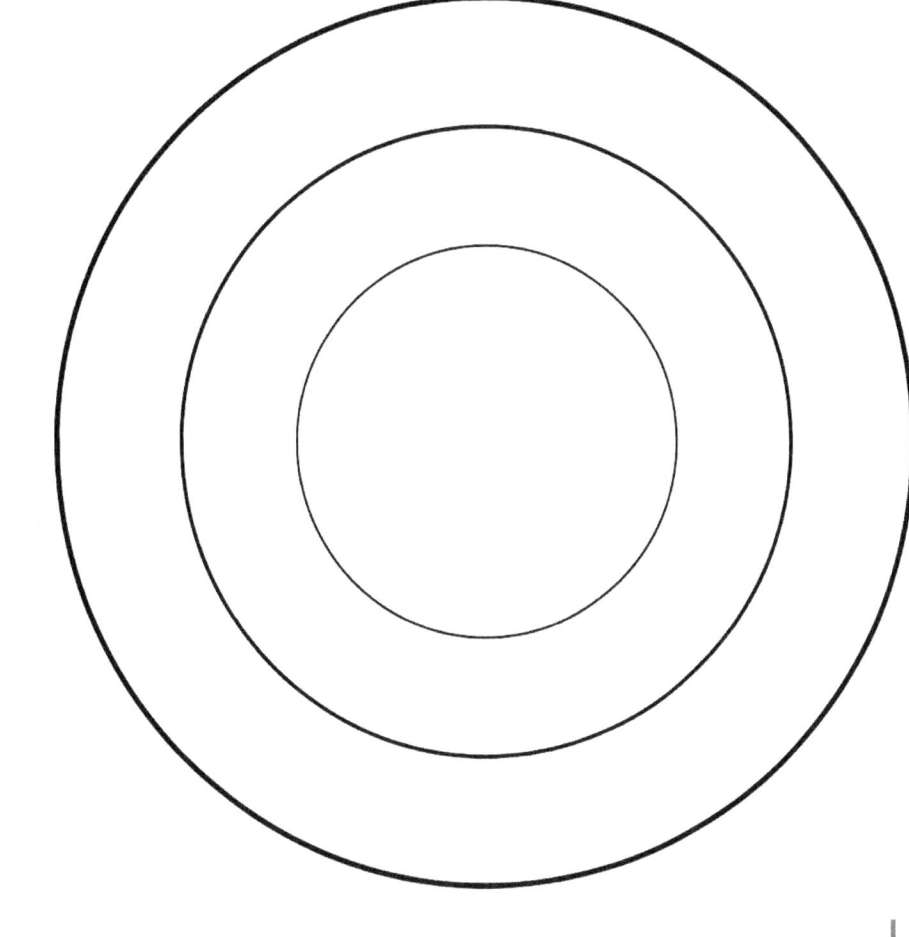

Let go to become empowered

After becoming aware of the circles of control, I felt a sense of empowerment that I hadn't experienced in years. As Covey suggested, I became proactive and less reactive. I realised how much time I had spent worrying or complaining about things beyond my control. I used to spend hours fretting over how a parent might respond to my email or what my colleagues thought of me. I also wasted precious energy complaining about new curriculum changes and blaming others for my lack of time to complete report cards. Once I let these worries go, I had more energy to focus on things I could actively control or influence. The to-do list may not get shorter, but by letting go of things you can't control, you increase your capacity to tackle it.

Asking for support during challenging classroom situations

While many stressors in teaching are beyond your control, how you respond to them is within your power. Teachers often navigate complex student behaviours – such as anxiety and anger – while witnessing distressing situations, including classroom disruptions, violent outbursts, self-harm and school refusal. These challenges require support from fellow educators and mental health professionals, yet many teachers hesitate to seek help or debrief after these difficult experiences.

During my conversations with school leaders and teachers, I have observed that teachers don't seek support or ask for help for a number of different reasons. Early-career teachers may fear appearing 'out of their depth', while experienced educators may worry about seeming 'inept'. This maladaptive belief – that asking for help is a sign of weakness – often leads to the suppression of uncomfortable emotions, unintentionally amplifying the nervous system's stress response. Over time, this can hinder your ability to remain regulated and prepared for unpredictable situations. Instead of internalising stress or believing you must handle everything alone, recognising when to ask for help is an act of strength, resilience and professional growth.

The importance of asking for help and how to do it effectively

Responding to critical incidents and behaviour challenges in the classroom with openness and support is essential for both teacher wellbeing and effective classroom management for the following reasons:

1. Teaching is unpredictable, and no educator has all the answers all the time. Acknowledging the challenges and reaching out for assistance allows teachers to navigate issues with greater confidence.
2. Suppressing emotions or blaming yourself for difficult situations can lead to burnout, anxiety and diminished confidence. Asking for help allows teachers to process challenges constructively and find solutions without internalising the stress.
3. When teachers openly ask for help, it normalises a culture of collaboration and emotional resilience. Colleagues may feel more comfortable seeking support themselves, strengthening trust and teamwork within the school.
4. Critical incidents often require collaboration. Consulting colleagues, school leaders or specialised staff can provide new insights, strategies and interventions that may not be immediately apparent when facing the issue alone.
5. Teachers are lifelong learners, and recognising when additional support is needed fosters professional development. Seeking advice, attending training sessions or working with mentors can enhance skills in managing difficult situations.

If asking for help makes you feel vulnerable or ashamed, some of the following conversation starters may help initiate a discussion with colleagues, school wellbeing professionals or leadership.

- *"I've been facing some challenges with [specific student behaviour or situation]. Could we talk through some strategies together?"*
- *"I'm struggling to process what just occurred. Could we debrief so I can better understand how to move forward?"*
- *"I'm realising I need some help navigating the stress that comes with certain classroom moments. Can we talk about ways to manage it?"*
- *"I think I could benefit from some additional guidance on [specific issue]. Would it be possible to have a chat about me engaging in some professional development in this area?"*

I recognise that seeking and receiving support is not always prioritised in schools. However, if you find yourself struggling without adequate support, I strongly encourage you to reach out to your Employee Assistance Program (EAP), school counsellor, colleague, school leader or wellbeing coordinator. Initiating a conversation to recognise staff mental health and wellbeing challenges, and emphasising the need for enhanced support processes, is a crucial first step towards meaningful change in schools. By actively seeking support and fostering open conversations, you can play a pivotal role in reducing the stigma around mental health, helping other teachers feel less isolated, and normalising the act of seeking help.

Establish your boundaries

Shifting your focus to the things you can control can provide you with additional mental and emotional space. However, there may be times when extra responsibilities or duties are assigned to you, necessitating the need to set boundaries. By establishing boundaries with yourself and others, you can be intentional about where you direct your time and energy. Establishing boundaries is particularly important for teachers. Many teachers share characteristics such as being highly capable, self-sacrificing and people-pleasing. As a result, overfunctioning is common among teachers, who are often praised for taking on others' duties, completing additional tasks and volunteering to help. While these actions are virtuous, self-sacrificing habits are unsustainable, leading to resentment, nervous system dysregulation and eventual burnout.

Learning how to say no

Learning to say no is a vital (and learnable) skill for teachers. In *Energy: Get it. Guard it. Give it.* (2024), O'Neill emphasises the importance of setting clear boundaries, encapsulated in the phrase, '"No" is a complete sentence'. She highlights that asserting oneself without justification fosters personal empowerment and energy preservation. As a reformed people-pleaser who once struggled to say no, I deeply appreciate this phrase. However, I also recognise how challenging it can be to set boundaries and confidently say no to others. That's why I've discovered that having a few intentional responses ready can make it easier to resist the urge to automatically say yes. These statements create space to pause, reflect and confidently set boundaries.

Figure 7.3: Setting boundaries

> # Boundaries:
> # State What You Want
>
> Use these phrases to practise saying what you want confidently and respectfully.
>
> - "I'd like to…"
> - "I'd prefer to…"
> - "I'd rather…"
> - "I want to…"
> - "I'm more comfortable with…"
> - "I've decided that…"
> - "I can only do this/meet on…"
> - "This is what's best for me…"
>
> NO FURTHER EXPLANATION IS REQUIRED WHEN STATING YOUR PREFERENCES & NEEDS

You deserve time for yourself

If you often find yourself taking on more than your fair share, you might initially feel guilty or uneasy about setting boundaries, fearing how others might react. Remember, while you can't manage others' reactions, you have full control over how you allocate your time and articulate your needs. In her book *Toxic Positivity* (2022), Whitney Goodman suggests the following statements for when you don't have the emotional or mental energy to give to others but want to offer your boundary in a gentle way:

- *"I'm sorry this is happening. I had a rough day and feel like I can't be the best support to you right now. Can I follow up with you in the next few days?"*
- *"I don't think I'm the best person to help you with that right now. Have you thought about reaching out to _____?"*

And remember, even if you have the time to take on additional tasks, it's OK to say no simply because you want to. You deserve time for yourself – it is not selfish. As I have reiterated throughout this book, teaching is emotionally and mentally draining. If you do not make changes to prioritise your mental health and wellbeing, you will eventually burn out.

Reflect: Ask yourself the following questions:

1. What personal and professional boundaries are important for you to maintain a healthy work-life balance?
2. How do you communicate your boundaries to colleagues, students and parents?
3. How do you handle situations where your boundaries are challenged or not respected?
4. What steps can you take to ensure you are focusing your energy on areas where you can make a difference?
5. How does focusing on your circles of control impact your overall wellbeing and effectiveness as a teacher?
6. What positive changes have you noticed when you concentrate on what you can control?

CHAPTER SUMMARY

- Teachers face constant challenges such as high workloads, parental demands, limited resources and administrative tasks, leaving little time to rest and recharge.
- While many stressors are beyond a teacher's control, managing personal energy, time, reactions and behaviours is key to reducing stress.
- Stephen Covey's 'circles of control' model emphasises focusing on what can be influenced, such as personal reactions, rather than external factors that cannot be changed.
- Setting boundaries helps teachers allocate their time and energy intentionally, avoiding overfunctioning behaviours that can lead to burnout.
- Saying no is a crucial skill for maintaining balance; statements can help gently enforce boundaries without guilt or overcommitment.
- Teachers must prioritise their mental health and wellbeing by recognising limits, setting boundaries and letting go of stressors they cannot control.

CHAPTER 8

Isn't it selfish to focus on myself rather than the students?

The positive impacts of practising self-regulation and self-compassion

"It takes courage to say yes to rest and play in a culture where exhaustion is seen as a status symbol" – Brené Brown

Take a moment to think about other teachers you know. It's likely you'll agree that most are self-sacrificing, highly capable and caring individuals. However, these traits can also lead to struggles with people-pleasing and perfectionism. I emphasise the word 'struggles' because these traits are unsustainable in the highly relational field of teaching. Speaking from experience, being both a people-pleaser and a perfectionist ultimately led me to burnout. I was so focused on 'getting it right', 'keeping the peace' and 'worrying about what others thought' in both my personal and professional life that it became unsustainable. To preserve my energy, I was pushed out of my window of tolerance, causing my nervous system to shift into hypo-arousal. I became withdrawn from colleagues, disillusioned by the system and unmotivated to teach. Although I didn't realise it at the time, I was essentially in shutdown mode and heading towards burnout.

Do you have the belief that you should prioritise others before yourself?

Like many people, especially women, I had the belief that taking time for myself was selfish because I had been conditioned by society to be caring, nurturing and selfless. On *The School of Wellbeing with Meg Durham* podcast (2024), guest Dr Michelle McQuaid explores the concept of the 'good girl' belief. In this episode Dr McQuaid emphasises how societal expectations shape behaviour, often encouraging individuals to prioritise pleasing others over asserting their own needs and boundaries. Dr McQuaid's qualitative research found that many women attain to 'good girl' beliefs, specifically believing that:

- We need to perform perfectly, but make it look effortless.
- We need to please everyone else and sacrifice our own wellbeing in the process.
- We need to protect everyone else – we need to silence our own emotional pain and needs so that we don't make other people feel uncomfortable or be seen as being too demanding.

Listening to Dr McQuaid's research findings was confronting but confirmed what I hear regularly from female teachers: "I know that much of my stress comes from my own pressure to be perfect." Additionally, in many schools, putting others first and not complaining is praised, while making time to rest and recharge is seen as selfish. Perhaps this is why the Be You and Beyond Blue *Mental Health in Education Report* (2024) states that high levels of stress, burnout and inadequate access to support are taking a toll on teachers, with only 38% indicating that they felt colleagues in their school were mentally healthy.

How can systems prioritise teacher wellbeing?

We need to change the narrative on what it means to be a 'good' teacher. Selflessly giving until the point of mental exhaustion and illness should not be praised and rewarded. In fact, school leaders should encourage teachers to take mental health days and celebrate teachers who prioritise having a lunch break. Promoting a culture which prioritises mental health and rest has many benefits, including:

- Reduced absenteeism
- Better retention rates
- Improved teacher-student relationships
- Increased creativity and job satisfaction

Unfortunately, many education systems around the world do not actively promote the collective wellbeing and mental health of teachers. Therefore, it's crucial to be proactive, prioritise your own wellbeing and remember that taking care of yourself is not selfish.

Reflect: Ask yourself the following questions:

1. Do you feel pressure to be perfect in your teaching? What are some specific areas where you feel this pressure?
2. How do you balance societal expectations with staying true to your authentic self as a teacher?
3. What qualities do you believe make a good teacher? How do these beliefs align with your teaching practice?
4. Who are the teachers or role models that have influenced your beliefs about what makes a good teacher? How do you incorporate their qualities and practices into your own teaching?
5. How do you define success as a teacher? What indicators do you use to measure your effectiveness?

Empower yourself by considering your choices

I loved 'choose your own adventure' books when I was younger. From reading so many of these books, I learned two important things:

1. In most situations, we have a choice.
2. Our choices and actions directly impact the outcome.

With that in mind, I want you to read the following scenario, consider the possible choices and reflect on the outcomes.

SCENARIO

After spending time speaking with some students after lessons, you rush out to your playground duty. Realising you forgot to bring lunch, you don't have time to get anything before heading to the playground. Standing in the hot sun, you help solve numerous lunchtime conflicts. Feeling hot, thirsty and hungry, you then rush straight back into the classroom for your next class.

CHOICE A

You enter the classroom feeling hungry, thirsty and irritable. Without taking a moment to connect with the students, you dive straight into the lesson content. Frustration builds as you notice the students are not ready to start learning, leading you to raise your voice multiple times. Startled by your outburst, a few students begin whispering to each other. In response, you express your frustration with their disrespectful behaviour and announce that the entire class will stay in for an additional five minutes.

(GO TO OUTCOME #2)

CHOICE B

As you enter the classroom, you inform the students that you haven't had lunch and are feeling quite hot. You emphasise the importance of staying hydrated and nourished for everyone's brains and bodies. You then send a student to the canteen to get you a cold drink and some lunch. You let the class know that they can chat quietly, draw or read while you take five minutes to eat and relax.

(GO TO OUTCOME #1)

OUTCOME #1

As you eat your lunch, you begin to feel calmer. The class is unusually quiet and seems content with the time you've given them to relax. One of your students approaches and asks if you feel better now that you've eaten. You feel grateful for having such kind students and become enthusiastic about starting the lesson. Energised throughout the lesson, you notice the students are engaged. As they leave the classroom, a few students thank you for giving them quiet time to relax after the hot lunchtime.

OUTCOME #2

Many students become upset and question why they are being punished when they haven't done anything wrong. The students remain restless and disengaged throughout most of the lesson, making it difficult for you to concentrate. At the end of the lesson, one student walks out of the class, yelling, "I'm not staying back because I didn't do anything wrong!" The rest of the class claps, leaving you feeling completely out of control.

Reflection:

Which outcome was better for the students?

Which outcome was better for you as the teacher?

Do you consider either of the choices to be selfish?

Who was disadvantaged by Choice A – the teacher, the students or both?

A regulated teacher fosters a regulated classroom

Taking actions to become regulated is not selfish, it is a choice which evidently results in better outcomes for you and your students. In his book *Building a Trauma-Informed Restorative School* (2020), Joe Brummer states that positivity and calmness are contagious. The more supportive and calm we become as staff, the more students feel safe and calm in our presence. Recent neuroscience research underscores this assumption: when teachers maintain emotional regulation, their students tend to follow suit. This alignment fosters stronger student-teacher relationships, greater student engagement and more effective classroom management.

In Episode 4 of his YouTube series *Stress, Trauma, and the Brain: Insights for Educators – Regulating Yourself and Your Classroom* (2020), Dr Bruce Perry highlights the vital importance of self-regulation for teachers and its profound influence on fostering a well-regulated classroom environment. He explains that when the teacher – the leader of the classroom – is dysregulated, overwhelmed, exhausted or frustrated, their cortex effectively shuts down, impairing their ability to teach students effectively. Dr Perry's research within education systems has demonstrated significant improvements in student cognitive and behavioural outcomes when schools support teachers, by providing breaks and respite for them to regulate.

Consequently, self-regulation is not only crucial for managing stress and maintaining your mental health and wellbeing, but it is also a powerful tool for creating a positive and productive classroom environment. Given the evident benefits for students, it seems unreasonable to think that taking time to become regulated could ever be considered selfish.

Learning to be compassionate with yourself

Seemingly, making time for self-regulation is beneficial for you personally and professionally. However, as human beings, there will be times when we are not regulated, make mistakes and have bad days. This is when the practice of self-compassion becomes particularly useful. Teachers excel at showing compassion to students, families and colleagues, but often struggle to extend that same compassion to themselves.

So, what is self-compassion?

Self-compassion means accepting that you are imperfect, instead of constantly criticising yourself for your weaknesses. Rather than listening to your inner critic and triggering your stress response, self-compassion triggers a soothing response in your nervous system. Leading psychologist in this field, Dr Kristen Neff (2011) defines self-compassion as entailing three main components which overlap and mutually interact: self-kindness, common humanity and mindfulness.

1. **Self-kindness** involves being caring and understanding towards yourself rather than being critical or judgemental. It is about providing comfort to yourself, instead of adopting a 'just grin and bear it' approach. This is especially important for teachers, who feel the need to prioritise everyone else's wellbeing over their own. Self-kindness can be as simple as the 'choose your own adventure' example – when you attend to your physiological needs by ensuring that you have had lunch, had a drink and been to the toilet!
2. **Common humanity** involves recognising that everyone fails, makes mistakes and feels inadequate at times. Teachers often feel isolated when reflecting on their personal flaws or mistakes, and this feeling is magnified when they compare themselves to other teachers. I remember feeling utterly hopeless during my first year of teaching as I compared myself to another Year 1 teacher who had been teaching for 20 years. Logically, the comparison was unreasonable and made me feel like a failure. Thankfully, I ended up sharing my feelings with her, and she empathised about the beginning years of teaching and explained that she still felt inadequate despite her years of experience.

   When we begin to understand that these experiences are a normal part of being a teacher and that other teachers share the same experiences and feelings of self-doubt and judgement, we experience common humanity. Common humanity encourages connection and empathy, reminding us that we are not alone in our experiences and face similar challenges. So, the next time you worry that your students are not progressing, that you must be a terrible teacher, and that every other teacher has it all figured out, reach out to other teachers in your team or join an online teaching group. You'll likely find that many others share similar feelings and are also 'just doing their best'.

3. **Mindfulness** involves being present in the moment, avoiding both ignoring and ruminating on aspects of yourself or your life. Before you can offer compassion to yourself, you must be aware of your emotions. Practising mindfulness helps teachers become more aware of their emotions and respond to challenging situations with greater composure and empathy (more on mindfulness practices in Chapter 11). Another significant benefit of mindfulness for teachers is that it reduces overidentification. Teachers are deep thinkers who are encouraged to reflect on their practice for continual improvement; however, this often leads to obsessive ruminating and negative self-talk. I was a constant overthinker during my initial years of teaching, but once I started practising mindfulness regularly, I noticed that I was more present and focused on my students and less critical of myself.

Prioritising yourself is not selfish

Selfishness is defined as prioritising your own needs, desires and interests above those of others. Consequently, prioritising your wellbeing through self-regulation and self-compassion cannot be considered selfish when these practices result in the following communal benefits:

✓ Enhanced student-teacher relationships
✓ Increased connection and solidarity among colleagues
✓ Greater engagement in teaching and learning
✓ A more positive and calmer classroom environment
✓ More effective responses to disruptive student behaviours

Reflect: Ask yourself the following questions:

1. How often do you find yourself being self-critical? What are some common self-critical thoughts you have? How can you reframe these thoughts to be more compassionate towards yourself?
2. How do you remind yourself to be kind and understanding towards yourself, especially on challenging days?
3. What changes have you noticed in your mood and energy levels when you are more self-compassionate?
4. Who in your life supports and encourages your practice of self-compassion?
5. What goals can you set to continue growing in your self-compassion practice?

CHAPTER SUMMARY

- Many teachers are self-sacrificing, highly capable and caring, but these traits can lead to struggles with people-pleasing and perfectionism, often resulting in burnout.
- Teachers, especially women, often feel conditioned to prioritise others over themselves, adhering to 'good girl' beliefs, such as perfect performance and suppressing emotional needs.
- A cultural shift is needed to prioritise teacher wellbeing, promoting mental health days, breaks and rest, which improve creativity, relationships and job satisfaction.
- Teachers maintaining emotional regulation foster a positive classroom environment, enhance student-teacher relationships and support better learning outcomes.
- Self-compassion involves self-kindness, recognising shared human experiences (common humanity) and mindfulness to reduce self-criticism and encourage emotional awareness.
- Practices like self-regulation and self-compassion benefit both teachers and their communities through stronger relationships, calmer environments and more effective teaching.

PART 3
SELF-REGULATION

DAILY PRACTICES TO REGULATE YOUR NERVOUS SYSTEM AND PRIORITISE YOUR MENTAL HEALTH AND WELLBEING

CHAPTER 9

How can I stay regulated when I am faced with challenges every day?

Create daily routines which prioritise your wellbeing and mental health

"Be the designer of your world and not merely the consumer of it" – James Clear

Throughout this book I suggest practices which help you regulate your nervous system and better manage stress, however, it's important to implement these practices even when you're not feeling stressed or overwhelmed. Doing so puts you in a better position to regulate your emotions in critical moments. By routinely engaging in activities that replenish your 'emotional tank', you can better access your emotional reserves to navigate challenging situations. This proactive investment in stress prevention helps you avoid emotional, mental and physical depletion, ensuring that you regularly renew your internal resources and enhance your overall wellbeing.

The emotional toll of teaching

Considering the amount of secondary traumatic stress (stress from supporting students impacted by traumatic experiences) and emotional demands that teachers are experiencing, it is necessary to be proactive in your efforts to regulate your nervous system and build your stress resilience.

The *Impact and Management of Secondary Trauma in Educators - Interim Report 2024* of Australian teachers found that:

- 61.4% report often or very often feeling overwhelmed with their workload
- 53% replay negative work events in their minds after leaving work, either often or very often
- 38% say that they experience secondary traumatic stress often or very often
- 75.3% agree that emotional demands impact their day to a large or very large extent

These emotional demands are significantly impacting teachers' ability to stay regulated. Essentially, the constant need to manage various student emotions and situations can deplete a teacher's emotional reserves, making it challenging to maintain emotional stability. As I have shared throughout this book, a teacher in a state of dysregulation does not have the capacity to manage their own emotions effectively, potentially leading to stress, burnout and decreased job performance if not properly addressed.

The benefits of self-regulation

The only thing you can control during challenging situations with students is your own nervous system. When a student is having a stress response and is in a flight or fight state, you cannot control their behaviour. During these times you may need to focus on self-preservation and the best way to do that is to manage your own stress. This enables you to respond in a regulated and composed manner, protecting your mental health and overall wellbeing. By maintaining a sense of calm while teaching, you create a stabilising presence that not only supports your own resilience but also fosters an environment that can help soothe and regulate a dysregulated student's stress response.

Nevertheless, maintaining emotional regulation is challenging, particularly if you lack self-regulation skills or feel unable to manage the stresses of your role. With the significant rise of student mental health issues and an increase in trauma-related behaviours in the classroom, teachers are increasingly expressing that they are not adequately trained to respond to the needs of these students. In addition, the rise of students diagnosed as neurodivergent necessitates specific supports and adjustments, which many teachers feel unprepared to implement effectively.

Brené Brown (2022) defines stress as "when we evaluate environmental demand as beyond our ability to cope successfully". This definition reflects the everyday challenges faced by many teachers who feel unprepared to meet the diverse needs of their students, often struggling to balance individualised support with the demands of the classroom. It also explains how ongoing overwhelm and uncertainty can dysregulate your nervous system, repeatedly pushing you beyond your window of tolerance and into states of hyper- or hypo-arousal. This persistent stress makes it harder to regain balance and regulate your emotional responses effectively. While essential training in trauma-informed practices and neurodiversity is needed within education systems, teachers can take proactive steps in the meantime to enhance their self-regulation skills, building resilience and fostering emotional balance.

By doing this you will be able to:

- Cope with the daily challenges and pressures of your role
- Improve student behaviour and engagement by creating a more positive and controlled classroom environment
- Better manage your emotions, reducing stress and preventing burnout
- Make more thoughtful and effective decisions, both in and out of the classroom

Reconnecting with your purpose can help establish positive habits

You can create new habits for improving self-regulation by developing your own routines. The first step in this process is deciding who you want to be. In *Atomic Habits* (2018), James Clear explains that most people begin the process of creating or changing habits by focusing on what they want to achieve. He suggests an alternative approach: start by focusing on who you wish to become.

Many teachers choose a career in education driven by a deep desire to make a meaningful impact on the lives of children and young people. While each educator's 'why' is unique, their passion and purpose often shine through when they reflect on their journey. Despite the challenges, teachers frequently express sentiments like:

- *"I love working with my students and seeing their incredible growth and progress."*
- *"Teaching has always felt more like a calling than a career – I knew this was my path from the start."*
- *"I was inspired by an amazing teacher who changed my life, and I want to do the same for others."*

Take a moment to reflect on your 'why' – the reasons you chose to become a teacher and the educator you aspire to be. James Clear suggests that when new routines and habits stem from a shift in identity, their impact extends beyond immediate results. Even if short-term rewards aren't immediately visible, maintaining a long-term vision of being a calm, engaging and connected teacher can provide the motivation to persist. As you begin to experience deeper relationships with students, reduced stress, a more positive mood and greater energy, your commitment to these habits will naturally strengthen.

Reflect: **Consider the following questions to deepen your understanding of your purpose and reconnect with your passion:**

1. What inspired you to become a teacher in the first place?
2. Can you recall a moment when you knew teaching was the right path for you?
3. In what ways do you continue to find joy and meaning in your work?
4. How do you want your students to remember you as a teacher?
5. What kind of impact do you want to have on your students' lives, both academically and personally?
6. How do you envision your ideal teaching self? What qualities and characteristics do you want to embody?

Assessing your current routines for regulation and wellbeing

The second step in the process is to identify your current routines and habits, then determine what changes are needed for improvement. Use Table 7 to assess your existing routines and pinpoint areas where new routines and habits are required.

Table 7: Wellbeing routines

Wellbeing routines	✓ ✗
Physical wellbeing routines:	
• I monitor how my movement impacts my mood.	☐
• I take movement breaks during my day (perhaps with students).	☐
• I stay hydrated throughout the day.	☐
• I take time to have rest breaks throughout the day without guilt.	☐
• I follow a nightly sleep routine.	☐
• I take time to eat breakfast and lunch during my workday.	☐
Mental wellbeing routines:	
• I take regular breaks from screens.	☐
• I automate certain work-related tasks (for example, sending automated reminders to parents or students).	☐
• I schedule time for silence and quiet every day.	☐
• I take brain breaks during my day.	☐
• I make time for self-reflection and de-briefing after stressful incidents.	☐
• I continuously seek to improve my competency and knowledge.	☐
• I often ask colleagues for help, wisdom or advice.	☐
Emotional wellbeing routines:	
• I recognise and monitor how different emotions show up in my body.	☐
• I engage in daily mindful breathing, meditation, or journalling practice.	☐
• I thoughtfully respond more than I negatively react to my emotions and the emotions of others.	☐
• I take time to reflect on my emotional responses to events and to other people.	☐
• I regularly make time to do things which bring me joy.	☐

Reflect: **After evaluating your daily wellbeing routines, take a moment to reflect on the following questions:**

1. **What daily routines do you have in place to support your overall wellbeing?**
2. **How do you incorporate activities that bring you joy and relaxation into your daily schedule?**
3. **What healthy habits have you established to support your wellbeing and stress management?**
4. **How do you ensure consistency in maintaining these healthy habits?**
5. **How do you reflect on your routines and habits to identify areas for improvement?**

Redesign your daily routines to promote regulation

The next few chapters of this book will introduce daily practices and techniques for regulating your nervous system and enhancing mental health and wellbeing. Many of these tools can be used during the school day to address feelings of stress and overwhelm, while others serve a preventative purpose. These routines provide a starting point, based on your current routine assessment, enabling you to plan more detailed routines tailored to your individual needs. Although the idea of adding more to your day might seem overwhelming, you can start small by incorporating one or two new routines into your daily schedule. This is how I began. Once I started to feel the overall improvement in my wellbeing, these routines evolved into habits that transformed my life, and now I couldn't imagine living without them.

Sticking to routines

Finding the energy and motivation to make meaningful life changes – such as establishing new routines – can be challenging. To support consistency and long-term success, the following strategies can help you stick to new routines and transform them into habits that bring lasting benefits for both yourself and your students.

1. **Streamline your routines with technology:** In today's modern world there are numerous ways that you can use technology to help stay consistent with your daily wellbeing routines and efficiently fit them into your day.
    - Set alarms and notifications on your phone or computer calendar to remind you of important routine tasks like exercise, meditation or gratitude practice.
    - Automate TV sleep timers and smartphone screen displays to turn off at a specific time, ensuring you adhere to your sleep routines.
    - Wear fitness-tracking devices such as Apple Watches or Fitbits to monitor your activity levels and remind you to move.
2. **Be accountable:** One of the best ways to stay on track with new routines is to find an accountability partner. Many years ago, I helped facilitate the NESLI Staff Wellbeing Toolkit at my school. One of the most popular aspects of the programme was sharing intentions with accountability buddies and checking in with each other. Teachers encouraged one another by going for walks together to improve physical wellbeing and offering opportunities for regular debriefs to enhance emotional wellbeing.
3. **Habit stack:** In *Atomic Habits* (2018), James Clear introduces the concept of 'habit stacking' as an effective method for creating new habits. Habit stacking involves identifying a habit you already perform daily and adding a new behaviour on top of it. For instance, if you want to establish a daily gratitude practice, you could set the intention to express gratitude every morning after pouring your coffee. The established habit of having your coffee will serve as a cue to remind you to practise gratitude.

Choosing up-regulating or down-regulating tools

Now that you understand the importance of establishing wellbeing routines and habits, you can select the tools that best suit your needs and integrate them into your daily life. Recognising whether your nervous system requires up-regulation or down-regulation depends on tuning in to your body's signals and energy levels.

Reflecting on Chapter 2, where Polyvagal Theory was explored, you now know that your nervous system operates in different states: relaxed, activated or immobilised. To determine whether you need up-regulating or down-regulating techniques, first identify whether you are in a state of activation (fight or flight) or shutdown (freeze). Once you recognise your nervous system state, select the appropriate tools to help restore balance and bring yourself back to a grounded, calm state. If you are experiencing dorsal vagal shutdown, gentle up-regulating techniques – such as mindful walking – can help reestablish a sense of safety and reconnection between mind and body. On the other hand, if you are in a sympathetic nervous system (SNS) state of fight or flight, down-regulating practices – such as the 5-4-3-2-1 grounding technique – can support relaxation and regulation.

Over the next three chapters I will introduce specific techniques and practices to help regulate your nervous system and manage stress, fostering greater balance and resilience. As you explore these tools, you'll gain confidence in selecting the methods that best support your wellbeing.

CHAPTER SUMMARY

- Regularly engage in activities that replenish your emotional reserves, even when not stressed, to build resilience and avoid emotional, mental and physical depletion.
- Teachers face significant emotional pressures, including secondary trauma and managing student emotions, which can deplete their ability to stay regulated.
- Regulating your nervous system during stress improves your mental health, maintains classroom composure and fosters a positive environment that enhances student behaviour and engagement.
- Developing stress-prevention routines starts by defining who you want to become and assess your current routines to identify changes needed for improving self-regulation and wellbeing.
- Streamline routines with tech tools like alarms, fitness trackers and accountability partners to stay consistent and effectively manage daily habits.
- Combine new habits with existing ones (for example, gratitude practice with morning coffee) to reinforce routines and make positive changes sustainable.
- Small routine changes, practised consistently, evolve into habits that improve overall wellbeing, helping you navigate daily challenges with greater ease.

CHAPTER 10

How can I manage stress when I am at school?

Daily exercises to use during the school day to discharge excessive stress energy

"Every time we experience stress, we have to burn energy to keep our internal systems running efficiently" – Stuart Shanker

Many people face stressors in their workplace, making work-related stress a common experience. However, the statistics presented in a 2023 Black Dog Institute report highlight the significant level of work-related stress experienced by teachers in comparison to the general population:

- 60% of teacher absences in the previous month [that research was conducted] were due to a mental health or emotional problem.
- 52% of teachers reported moderate to extremely severe symptoms of depression compared to 12.1% in the general population.
- 46.2% of teachers reported anxiety symptoms compared to 9% in the general population.
- 59.7% of teachers reported experiencing stress compared to 11.4% in the general population.

Releasing built-up stress benefits you and your students

Recognising and managing workday stress is crucial to avoid nervous system dysregulation. Classroom stressors causing anger, frustration or panic typically trigger the fight or flight response, circulating stress energy throughout the body and even impacting those around you. In his book *Building a Trauma-Informed Restorative School* (2020), Joe Brummer describes how our stress levels as adults impact our students:

> *"They are looking to us to help give them a sense of safety. When they sense we are stressed out, their nervous system reacts to our stress. When they sense our anxiety, they become anxious with us. Even if you think you've put the best smile on you can, it won't help. The brain's stress response threat-detection system doesn't tend to fall for tricks."*

Thankfully, when you start to feel tension and stress in your body, you can release the stress by engaging in somatic (body) exercises. These exercises allow your muscles to physically discharge some of the stress energy. This helps to complete the stress response cycle and in turn regulates your nervous system. Consequently, a regulated nervous system not only benefits you personally but can also positively influence your students, who are likely to reflect your calm and composed state by becoming more settled themselves.

Techniques for discharging stress energy

In Chapter 5 I stated that discharging stress energy through physical activity is the most effective way to tell your brain that you have successfully survived a threat, and that your body can relax. In *The Vagus Nerve Reset* (2023), Anna Ferguson explains that bottom-up approaches, such as somatic exercises, begin with the body – its sensations and movements – rather than the mind. These techniques rely on sensory input from both external and internal environments, helping the body signal to the brain whether it is in a state of safety or threat. By using bottom-up methods to access stored emotions and release stress energy, you expand your capacity to engage cognitive (top-down) processes more effectively.

Surprisingly simple to practise, somatic exercises offer profound and powerful benefits. In his book *The Power of Now* (2001), Eckhart Tolle describes the release of surplus energy through body movement as 'natural wisdom'. He shares the following story to highlight the significance of this process:

> "Occasionally two ducks will get into a fight... The fight usually lasts only for a few seconds, and then the ducks separate, swim off in opposite directions, and vigorously flap their wings a few times. They then continue to swim on peacefully as if the fight had never happened. When I observed that for the first time, I suddenly realised that by flapping their wings, they were releasing surplus energy, thus preventing it from becoming trapped in their body and turning into negativity."

Alongside somatic exercises, breathing techniques serve as powerful tools for transitioning out of a heightened sympathetic nervous system state. When rapid breathing signals the brain to enter an alert, survival mode, these practices help restore a sense of calm and regulation. By completing these exercises during your day, you are ensuring that the stress response cycle has been completed, and stress is not lingering in your body. These exercises and techniques can be incorporated into your daily routine – whether in the classroom with students, during playground duty, over lunch or at the end of the day. The timing isn't what matters most; what's important is making space for stress-relief practices to prevent tension from accumulating in your body.

Tools for discharging stress energy at work

#1 Push on a wall

Pushing against a wall is a somatic exercise that helps release stress by engaging the body in deep-pressure stimulation, which can regulate the nervous system and promote relaxation. Stress often manifests as muscle tightness – pushing against a wall engages multiple muscle groups, allowing for controlled tension release.

1. Place your palms on a wall with your arms extended.
2. Bend your elbows and plant your feet firmly on the floor.
3. Push against the wall as hard as you can for 10–20 seconds and repeat if needed.

#2 Somatic shaking

Somatic shaking is a powerful technique for releasing stress and tension by engaging the body's natural ability to discharge built-up energy. It involves rhythmic, spontaneous movements that help reset the nervous system and promote relaxation.

1. Stand with your feet hip-width apart, knees slightly bent and arms relaxed at your sides.
2. Begin gently shaking your hands and wrists, and gradually move the shaking to your arms, shoulders, torso and legs.
3. Focus on breathing deeply through your nose and exhaling through your mouth as you shake your limbs.
4. Continue shaking for as long as you need to feel the energy moving through your body (approximately 3–5 minutes).
5. When you feel ready, start to slow down the shaking and gradually go still.

#3 Progressive muscle relaxation

Progressive muscle relaxation is a powerful technique for reducing stress by systematically tensing and relaxing different muscle groups in the body. This practice helps release physical tension, calm the nervous system and promote emotional regulation.

1. Sit on a chair and take a long, deep breath in and out.
2. Begin by tensing a muscle group for 5–10 seconds (i.e. clench your hands tightly to make fists).
3. Exhale slowly and release the tension.
4. Relax the muscle for 10–20 seconds.
5. Repeat the process with the next muscle group.
6. Move through your body, tensing and releasing each muscle group.
7. Focus on the tension and relaxation of each muscle group.

#4 Vigorous movement

Intense physical activity stimulates the release of endorphins – the brain's natural feel-good chemicals – and regular movement prevents chronic stress build-up and supports emotional resilience.

1. Choose a movement and intentionally timetable it into your day:
   - Walk briskly around your designated playground duty area.
   - Join a colleague for a lunchtime walk (possibly to the local café for a coffee).
   - Run on the spot for three minutes or do 10 star jumps.
   - Take your students for a brisk walk or run.
   - Take your dog for a walk after work.
   - Go for a swim after work.
   - Dance to your favourite music.
2. Focus on the tension and stress energy releasing from your body as you move.

#5 Physiological sigh

The physiological sigh is a simple yet powerful breathing technique that helps reduce stress by quickly calming the nervous system. This breathing pattern has been shown to effectively lower stress and anxiety by shifting the body from a sympathetic (fight or flight) state to a parasympathetic (rest and digest) state.

1. Inhale deeply through your nose.
2. Without exhaling, take another quick, deep breath in through your nose to fully expand your lungs.
3. Exhale slowly and fully through your mouth, emptying your lungs completely.
4. Repeat one or two more times.

#6 Use a stress ball

Squeezing a stress ball activates muscles in the hand and forearm, helping to release stored tension. The rhythmic contraction and relaxation of muscles can promote a sense of physical relief.

1. Place the stress ball in the palm of your hand.
2. Gently squeeze the stress ball, applying pressure with your fingers and palm.
3. Slowly release the pressure, allowing the stress ball to return to its original shape.
4. Continue squeezing and releasing the stress ball for a few minutes, focusing on the sensation in your hand and the rhythm of your breathing.

#7 Use a stretch resistance band

Resistance band* exercises help stretch and activate muscles, reducing built-up tension and stress in the body. Focusing on movement rather than stressors helps redirect anxious energy into productive physical activity.

1. Stand with your feet shoulder-width apart and hold the resistance band with both hands, palms facing down.
2. Extend your arms out in front of you straight, keeping them at shoulder height.
3. Gently pull the band apart as you squeeze your shoulder blades together.
4. You should feel the stretch in your chest and front shoulders.
5. Do 20–30 reps for 2–3 sets.

*Affordable resistance bands are available at Kmart, making them a budget-friendly option for discharging stress energy.

Reflect: **Ask yourself the following questions:**

1. What tools or techniques do you currently use to manage stress in the classroom? How effective do you find these tools in helping you stay calm and focused?
2. What physical activities or exercises do you use to release stress during the school day?
3. How do you incorporate movement or physical breaks into your routine to manage stress?
4. Do you practise mindfulness or meditation to help manage stress?
5. What goals can you set to continue developing your ability to manage and release stress effectively?
6. Which suggestions from this chapter would you like to try?

CHAPTER SUMMARY

- Recognising and managing daily stress is crucial to prevent nervous system dysregulation, which can lead to emotional and physical strain.
- Techniques like somatic exercises help complete the stress response cycle, allowing the body to discharge stress energy and return to a regulated state.
- Somatic stress-relief techniques such as pushing on a wall, somatic shaking and progressive muscle relaxation physically release tension and stress energy.
- Activities like brisk walking, running, dancing or swimming can effectively dissipate stress energy and promote relaxation.
- Controlled breathing techniques like the physiological sigh regulate the nervous system by signalling safety and reducing the stress response.
- Incorporating stress-relief techniques into your daily routine – whether in the classroom, during playground duty, lunch breaks or at the end of the day – helps prevent stress build-up and supports overall wellbeing.

CHAPTER 11

How can I stop my mind from constantly overthinking?

Mindfulness techniques to reduce feelings of overwhelm and help you relax

"Peace comes from within. Do not seek it without" – Buddha

Teaching demands daily engagement in a multitude of mental tasks, including planning, questioning, observing, reviewing, assessing, negotiating, organising and decision-making – just to name a few! These tasks demand significant cognitive effort, mental energy and focus, often leading to overthinking to ensure nothing is overlooked. My mind often felt so overstimulated that if I had to make one more decision or answer another question, it felt like my brain would explode. Do you ever feel this way?

The only thing which ever worked to quieten my mind was when I started practising mindfulness. Neuroscientist Stan Rodski states that mindfulness can be thought of as a rest from the busy activity of our brain. That is what mindfulness practice feels like for me – pressing pause on the internal chatter while I focus all my attention on one thing. It's incredibly freeing to be able to focus on just *one* thing for a while. I still remember attending my first yoga class and the instructor saying, "Get comfortable on your mat.

No one needs you. You have nowhere else to be and nothing else to do but be here in the present moment." I vividly remember questioning if this was true – could I genuinely give myself permission to stop? Since that day, I've made yoga a regular practice because I know my mind needs it.

Nonetheless, mindfulness doesn't have to be limited to yoga classes or meditation sessions. In his book *The Neuroscience of Mindfulness* (2018), Rodski states that mindfulness involves paying attention to something, in a particular way, on purpose, in the present moment, non-judgementally. Mindfulness is not one-size-fits-all. As long as you follow the process of paying attention to what you're doing while you're doing it and returning your attention to the task at hand if you notice your mind wandering, you are practising mindfulness. Therefore, the following daily activities and hobbies can help you cultivate mindfulness.

Mindfulness in action: Daily activities and hobbies

- Knitting
- Gardening
- Colouring in
- Jigsaw puzzles
- Cooking
- Painting or drawing
- Photography
- Lego and model construction
- Sewing
- Fishing

As I compiled this list, I was reminded of how many of these activities I enjoyed as a child, and how they are less common for children today. Perhaps spending more time on mindful hobbies that require attention, creativity and concentration could help both children and adults become more regulated.

Benefits of mindfulness

A key aspect of mindfulness is helping you develop skills to handle the demanding, challenging and stressful situations involved with teaching. Functional MRI studies have demonstrated that individuals who practise mindfulness exhibit reduced reactivity to emotional stimuli and enhanced emotional regulation during stressful situations. An increasing amount of research highlights the numerous benefits of mindfulness practice for teachers, including:

1. **Emotional regulation:** Mindfulness assists teachers in understanding and managing their emotions, decreasing stress and preventing burnout.
2. **Classroom management:** Employing mindfulness techniques can assist educators in addressing challenging student behaviours with greater calmness and efficacy.
3. **Stress reduction:** Regular mindfulness practice can lower cortisol levels, reducing stress and anxiety.
4. **Focus and attention:** Practising mindfulness enhances teachers' focus and presence, thereby improving their teaching performance.

Evidently, incorporating mindfulness into daily routines can enrich the classroom environment, providing positive outcomes for teachers and students.

Benefits for you and your students

Experiencing many of these practices alongside your students not only ensures they are integrated into your daily schedule but also provides mutual benefits for both you and your students. For example, mindful walking is an easy and effective practice to engage in with students of all ages. I have found that younger students love walking silently through outdoor spaces, intently listening for different sounds. This three-minute practice calms them as they focus on their senses and become mindful of their surroundings. Similarly, I have encouraged energetic, older students to join mindful walks with the goal of silently counting their steps. When you join your students in this experience, you will feel more relaxed and benefit from the calming effect that this mindfulness practice has on them.

Reduce stress by prioritising mindfulness

By focusing on the present moment and releasing stressors, mindfulness plays a crucial role in deactivating the sympathetic nervous system and activating the parasympathetic nervous system – promoting relaxation and reducing stress. While the benefits of mindfulness are vast, many teachers struggle to find space for these practices amid the chaos and demands of a busy school day, leading to a build-up of stress. Prioritising mindfulness can be achieved through intentional approaches, such as integrating mindfulness exercises into the daily schedule and creating dedicated mindfulness spaces within classrooms or schools.

Mindfulness/regulation spaces for teachers

Just as calming environments help children regulate their nervous systems, teachers also benefit from access to quiet, restorative spaces. As we explored in Chapter 6, teaching demands significant mental and emotional energy. The most effective way to replenish these reserves is by intentionally creating space and granting yourself permission to pause and rest. Despite the need for respite, traditional staffrooms often fall short in fostering mindfulness and supporting teachers' emotional regulation throughout the school day. School leaders who understand the science-backed advantages of mindfulness may explore the potential benefits of establishing regulation spaces where teachers can unwind without noise and distraction. Simple tools – such as headphones for music or guided meditations, books for colouring, pulse oximeters to regulate breath and fidget tools for sensory focus – can aid in lowering cortisol levels. Even a brief five-minute visit to such a space can have a profound impact, fostering a sense of balance and wellbeing.

If these spaces are not available in your school, you can always create your own space to reset. In Meg Durham's *School of Wellbeing* podcast (2024), Lisa O'Neill shared a story about encouraging a woman to create a 'car picnic' during her workday after realising she wasn't taking lunch breaks. Inspired by the idea, the woman embraced it fully – purchasing a picnic basket, vibrant plates and cups, and a thermos. Each day, she retreated to her car at lunchtime, where she enjoyed music, a podcast or simply the peacefulness of solitude. Even practising this small ritual a few times a week could lead to a noticeable boost in your energy levels and overall wellbeing.

With all these potential benefits, you're likely eager to integrate mindfulness into your daily routine – seamlessly and without it consuming too much of your valuable time. You can engage with the following practices whenever it suits you. Most of the practices take less than five minutes, so you can try them before school, throughout the day, during your lunch break or at the end of the day. Some particular practices such as mindful colouring or body scan may also be best practised at night when your mind is overthinking and you want to relax.

Mindfulness practices to help you relax

#1 Five-finger breathing

Five-finger breathing is a simple yet powerful mindfulness technique that combines deep breathing with tactile awareness to promote relaxation and emotional regulation. It's especially effective for reducing stress and anxiety because it engages multiple senses, helping to anchor you in the present moment.

1. Hold one hand out like you are giving a high five – this is your base hand. Use your other hand as your tracing hand.
2. Place the index finger of your tracing hand at the bottom of the thumb of your base hand.
3. Slowly move your index finger up to the tip of your thumb and take a deep breath.
4. Trace the index finger down the other side of your thumb as you breathe out.
5. Repeat with each finger, moving up the hand as you breathe in and down as you breathe out.
6. When you've traced your whole hand and reached the bottom of your pinky finger, reverse directions and follow the process, moving towards your thumb.
7. Remember to breathe slowly and focus on the sensation of your index finger touching your skin.

#2 Mindful walking

Mindful walking, also known as walking meditation, is a practice that combines movement with present-moment awareness. Instead of walking on autopilot, you intentionally focus on each step, your breath and the sensations in your body, creating a deep sense of connection with yourself and your surroundings.

1. Before starting, decide what you want to focus on during your walk, like simply observing your surroundings or focusing on a particular sense, for example, what you can hear.
2. Choose a place where you can walk outdoors and experience nature.
3. Take a few deep breaths to centre yourself and connect with your body.
4. Notice the sensation of your feet hitting the ground with each step, feeling the weight distribution and movement.
5. Actively observe what you see, hear, smell and feel around you.
6. Walk slowly for deeper observation.

#3 Box breathing

Box breathing is a powerful mindfulness tool that helps regulate the nervous system, reduce stress and enhance focus.

1. Sit comfortably. Close your eyes if you feel comfortable.
2. Breathe in slowly to the count of four.
3. Hold your breath for the count of four.
4. Exhale slowly and deeply to the count of four.
5. Hold your breath for the count of four.
6. Repeat the process several more times as you essentially visualise breathing around the sides of a square.

#4 Mindful colouring

Mindful colouring is a relaxing and meditative practice that involves focusing on the act of colouring with full awareness and presence. It encourages you to engage with the process rather than the outcome, helping to reduce stress, enhance focus and promote emotional regulation.

1. Choose any image you want to colour and select colouring pens.
2. Set aside 5-10 minutes to focus on colouring (you do not need to finish the whole picture).
3. Choose a colour and begin colouring.
4. Focus on your breathing, the design, your colour choices and the process of colouring.
5. Try not to judge your colouring but instead be present and aware of what you're doing.
6. If your mind wanders, gently bring your attention back to the image you are colouring.

#5 Listen to music

Listening to music can be a powerful tool for relaxation, mindfulness and emotional regulation. It engages multiple areas of the brain, stimulating the nervous system in ways that promote calmness and reduce stress.

1. Put headphones on (if possible) as they block out distractions.
2. Choose music which helps you to feel calm. Low pitch and slow tempo are recommended.
3. Search for meditation music, nature sounds or binaural beats to aid relaxation.
4. Listen for a minimum of 20 minutes as research shows that this reduces stress.

#6 Body scan

A body scan mindfulness practice is a meditation technique that helps you develop awareness of physical sensations, release tension and cultivate a deeper connection between your mind and body. It involves systematically bringing attention to different areas of the body, noticing any sensations, discomfort or relaxation without judgement.

1. Sit in a relaxed, upright position.
2. Take a few deep breaths and close your eyes (if it is suitable).
3. Focus your attention on your head, scanning your scalp, forehead, eyes and facial features.
4. Slowly move your awareness down your body, paying attention to your neck, shoulders, arms, hands, chest, stomach, hips, legs and feet.
5. Notice any physical sensations like tension, warmth or pain in each area.
6. Acknowledge any sensations that arise. Say 'relax' in your mind as you breathe deeply and let go of the tension.
7. End your scan by focusing on your feet and toes, taking a few final deep breaths.

7 Bilateral stimulation (thigh and finger taps)

These tools are useful as they are discreet. Bilateral stimulation can be done while sitting at your desk or behind your back.

Thigh taps:

1. Place your hands on your thighs and begin to tap back and forth, one side at a time.
2. Keep the rhythm slow and steady like your heartbeat.
3. Slow down your breathing and focus on your inhales and exhales.

Finger taps:

1. Bring your arms behind your back, crossing them over at the wrists.
2. Gently alternate tapping your thumb against your pointer and middle finger, switching between your left and right hands.
3. Slow down your breathing and focus on your inhales and exhales.

#8 The 'What Went Well' gratitude practice

The 'What Went Well' exercise, also known as 'Three Good Things', is a gratitude practice developed by Dr Martin Seligman, a pioneer in positive psychology. This exercise helps shift your focus from negative experiences to positive ones, promoting a more optimistic outlook on life. By reflecting on and appreciating three good things that happened during your day, you cultivate a mindful awareness of the positive aspects of your life, which can enhance overall wellbeing.

1. Dedicate 5-10 minutes each day to engage in the practice, ideally before bed or at the end of your workday.
2. Think about three things that went well during your day. These can be big achievements or small pleasures.
3. Record these three positive events by writing them down in a journal or on a piece of paper.
4. For each positive event, reflect on why it happened and what it means to you. An example entry may be: *I had a great conversation with my colleague today. It went well because I made an effort to listen actively and share my own experiences.*
5. Do this exercise consistently for at least a week, but aim for longer to see more significant benefits.

Reflect: Ask yourself the following questions about your mindfulness practice:

1. Are there moments in your teaching day when you feel disconnected or overwhelmed? Which mindfulness techniques do you think might help in those moments?
2. How do you currently practise mindfulness in your daily life?
3. What mindfulness techniques do you find most effective for managing stress?
4. How has mindfulness influenced your emotional resilience and ability to handle challenges?
5. Has practising mindfulness affected your ability to maintain a work-life balance?
6. What new mindfulness strategies or resources would you like to explore to further improve your wellbeing?

CHAPTER SUMMARY

- Teachers engage in numerous mental tasks daily, often leading to overstimulation, overthinking and mental exhaustion.
- Mindfulness practices act as a pause for the brain, helping teachers focus on the present moment, quiet internal chatter and reduce stress.
- Everyday hobbies like knitting, gardening, colouring or photography can cultivate mindfulness by requiring attention, creativity and concentration.
- Mindfulness promotes emotional regulation, reduces stress, improves classroom management, enhances focus and lowers cortisol levels.
- Mindfulness helps deactivate the sympathetic nervous system and activate the parasympathetic nervous system, fostering calm and relaxation.
- Practices like five-finger breathing, mindful walking, box breathing, colouring, listening to calming music or body scans can be seamlessly integrated into daily routines for stress relief.

CHAPTER 12

What can I do when I feel overwhelmed, anxious or have a panic attack?

Techniques to stimulate your vagus nerve and promote relaxation

"Take a deep breath and let it all go" - Oprah Winfrey

There is no doubt that teaching can be stressful. However, certain situations or experiences may escalate from being merely stressful to overwhelming, triggering a physiological survival response. This may lead to symptoms such as trembling, a rapid heartbeat, nausea and shortness of breath. Fortunately, the vagus nerve plays a key role in counterbalancing the fight or flight response, activating relaxation and promoting a sense of calm. However, when vagal tone is low, it can be harder to regulate emotions, making it more difficult to recover from anxiety or panic episodes. Strengthening vagal tone through intentional practices can enhance overall emotional resilience. This chapter will investigate techniques for stimulating your vagus nerve and improving your vagal tone to protect you during times of extreme overwhelm and panic.

What is the vagus nerve and how can you improve vagal tone?

The vagus nerve is the longest cranial nerve running from the base of the skull to the intestines. It has been referred to as an information superhighway because it is a bidirectional system, either carrying signals from the body to the brain or from the brain to the body.

As a component of the parasympathetic nervous system (PNS), the vagus nerve plays a crucial role in regulating our nervous system. When activated, it functions like the brake pedal in a car, slowing down our heart and breathing rates, decreasing blood pressure, facilitating digestion and promoting relaxation. Conversely, when the vagus nerve is deactivated, it allows the sympathetic nervous system to dominate, triggering the fight or flight response.

Thankfully, we can stimulate our vagus nerve to send a message to our bodies that it's time to relax and de-stress. The most effective way for this to occur is when we have good vagal tone. Vagal tone is an internal biological process that indicates the activity of the vagus nerve. In her book *The Vagus Nerve Reset* (2023), Anna Ferguson describes vagal tone as a measure of how well your vagus nerve is functioning, indicating your ability to recover from stress. Essentially, vagal tone reflects the state of your nervous system. High vagal tone is associated with a better ability to manage stress and anxiety by promoting relaxation, while a low vagal tone indicates increased stress reactivity and potential for heightened anxiety symptoms.

Techniques to stimulate your vagus nerve

By practising these techniques, you are stimulating the vagus nerve, which functions as an 'off switch' for stress. This helps establish calming effects, reduce anxiety and improve emotional regulation. These techniques can be effective for managing stress, anxiety or panic attacks and can be used during or immediately after an occurrence to help reduce symptoms and regain control.

How vagus nerve techniques have impacted my wellbeing

I have personally found cold exposure to be highly effective during a panic attack, providing immediate relief. Additionally, yoga and chanting have been powerful tools in promoting a deep sense of calm and emotional balance. In my late teens and early 20s, I regularly experienced panic attacks. However, after developing a better understanding of them and increasing my self-awareness, I had not had an attack for more than 20 years – until two years ago.

While sitting in a café with a friend, I received some distressing news. As I felt the familiar sensations of nausea, rapid heartbeat, sweating and shortness of breath, I immediately realised I was having a panic attack. Knowing logically that it would pass, I tried to slow my breathing and repeated "I am safe" in my mind. Despite my efforts, the panic did not subside. Thankfully, my friend asked the café for some ice and I placed it on the back of my neck. The sense of calm that washed over me was almost instant. My breathing returned to normal and the nausea disappeared. I felt calm.

I've practised yoga for more than 15 years and often tell others how it's one of the few things that truly quiets the mental chatter in my mind and eases the tension in my body. My sister, however, was initially sceptical about its benefits and not confident enough to join a yoga class. Instead of attending a class she opted to try a few online yoga sessions. It didn't take long before she noticed her body and mind relaxing, and after gaining confidence through these sessions, she eventually decided to join a local yoga group. Needless to say, she now shares her positive experience of yoga with others, just as I do. The message of this story is that it's OK to give new things a try by starting where you feel comfortable.

I can also personally attest to the calming effects of stimulating your vagus nerve through chanting. Last year, while reading Sonia Choquette's book *Trust Your Vibes* (2010), she suggested how powerful Om chanting can be to promote a sense of inner calm and peace. She suggested that just a few minutes of breathing in and exhaling a slow *om* sound could be transformative, so I gave it a try. The first time I tried it, it felt a bit strange, but I was pleasantly surprised by how relaxed I felt afterwards. The next few times I practised Om chanting, I experienced an instant feeling of inner peace and calm that lasted throughout the day. Recently, I read a study that showed chanting "om" deactivates the limbic centre of the brain, which is responsible for processing threats and emotions. I was amazed to find scientific evidence supporting what I had felt! Now, whenever I feel panicky, on edge or overwhelmed, I sit down and do Om chanting for a few minutes.

These are my personal experiences with vagus nerve practices. While they may not work the same for everyone, I am sharing the following techniques in the hope that you find one that suits your personal needs.

Vagus nerve techniques

The following evidence-based techniques are designed to stimulate the vagus nerve, promoting the PNS ventral vagal pathway. Certain methods are particularly effective for responding to stress and anxiety, while others serve as preventative measures to enhance vagal tone. For instance, you might find the 5-4-3-2-1 grounding technique easy to practise during the school day when feeling stressed, whereas diaphragmatic breathing might be your go-to relaxation method before bedtime. Regardless of which technique you choose, activating your relaxation response will calm your body and mind.

#1 Cold exposure

Cold exposure has been proven to regulate the nervous system because it lowers stress hormones. When your face comes in contact with cold water, it activates the body's natural response to conserve oxygen – thus slowing down your heart rate. Cold exposure can be performed in several ways, so you can choose which works best for you.

Have a cold shower: Keep the water temperature cold throughout your entire shower or switch to cold for the last few minutes to give yourself a refreshing blast.

Cold-water plunge: Immerse yourself in a cold pool, bath or body of water. This activity has become very popular with athletes and within the wellness industry for its numerous benefits.

Use ice: Run an ice cube over your wrists, neck or chest or hold a frozen icepack to the back of your neck for 30–60 seconds.

Cold-water facial: Splash cold water on your face or dunk your face in a bowl of cold water. Repeat a few times.

#2 Vocalising (humming, chanting or singing)

Scientific studies have demonstrated that when we sing, hum or chant, the vibrations of our vocal cords stimulate the vagus nerve. This is because the vagus nerve runs through your neck alongside your larynx and pharynx. Try one of the following vocalising activities to stimulate and tone your vagus nerve:

- Sing or hum your favourite song.
- Bee breathing (humming): Inhale deeply through your nose. As you exhale, gently hum, sounding like *mmmmmm*. Feel the vibration in your chest, throat and head. Repeat three or four times.
- Chanting 'om': Sit comfortably, take a deep breath and chant "om" as you exhale. Feel the vibrations resonate around your ears. Repeat this process at least five times or for as long as you need.

#3 Grounding technique – 5-4-3-2-1

This technique is highly versatile as it can be practised anywhere and anytime. Performing it helps disrupt the cycle of anxious thoughts by diverting your focus to the sensations in your body in the present moment. It helps ground you by engaging your senses to notice your current experience.

- Name **5** things you can see (for example, your laptop, the trees outside your window).
- Name **4** things you can feel (for example, the cool breeze on your face, your clothes).
- Name **3** things you can hear (for example, birds chirping, children's voices).
- Name **2** things you can smell (for example, coffee, food cooking).
- Name **1** thing you can taste (for example, your lunch, water or toothpaste).

#4 Diaphragmatic breathing (also known as belly breathing)

Slow, deep breathing activates the vague nerve, resulting in a decrease in anxiety and stress responses.

1. Inhale slowly through your nose, paying attention to the sensation.
2. Focus on your belly rising and falling with each breath (you may want to put your hands on your belly to feel the rise and fall).
3. Exhale slowly through your mouth, ensuring the exhale is at least two to three times as long as the inhale.
4. Relax your neck and shoulders as you continue to breathe deeply.

#5 Mindfulness meditation

Mindfulness meditation is a practice that involves focusing your attention on the present moment, while calmly acknowledging and accepting your feelings, thoughts and bodily sensations. Regular meditation practices, such as mindfulness, have been shown to enhance the health and activity of the vagus nerve, which plays a crucial role in regulating stress and promoting relaxation.

1. **Find a quiet space:** Choose a comfortable, distraction-free environment where you can sit or lie down. Keep your spine straight but relaxed.
2. **Set an intention:** Decide what you want to focus on – whether it's relaxation, emotional awareness or simply being present.
3. **Focus on your breath:** Close your eyes and take slow, deep breaths. Inhale through your nose, hold briefly and exhale gently through your mouth. Let your breath flow naturally.
4. **Observe your thoughts without judgement:** Your mind may wander – that's normal. Instead of resisting thoughts, simply notice them and gently bring your focus back to your breath.
5. **Engage your senses:** Notice the sensations in your body, the feeling of air moving in and out, or any sounds around you. Stay present with whatever arises.

6. **Use a mantra or visualisation (optional):** If helpful, repeat a calming phrase (such as "I am at peace") or visualise a peaceful scene, like waves gently rolling onto the shore.
7. **End with gratitude:** After a few minutes, slowly bring awareness back to your surroundings. Wiggle your fingers and toes, stretch gently and take a final deep breath. Express gratitude for taking this time for yourself.

If practising meditation independently feels challenging, you can use a meditation app or listen to a guided meditation to help you stay focused and engaged. Guided sessions provide structure, soothing instructions and techniques to ease you into mindfulness, making the practice more accessible and supportive.

#6 Yoga

Yoga integrates breathwork and movement, both of which stimulate the vagus nerve. Although some people still think of yoga as 'a bit woo woo', the research tells us that this holistic practice fosters deep relaxation and improves stress resilience. The beauty of yoga is that it's a personal practice which allows you to participate at your pace, in your way. If you are not ready to join a yoga class, you can follow a free yoga video on YouTube or follow visual instructions on the internet. Even just practising one or two postures for a few minutes a day can have a major impact. For example, the tree pose helps you focus inwards, quietening racing thoughts.

To do a tree pose:

1. From standing, support your weight with your right foot and slowly lift your left foot off the ground.
2. Slowly turn the sole of your left foot towards the inside of your right leg.
3. Place it on your right ankle, calf or thigh (avoid pressing your foot into your knee).
4. Rest your arms by your sides, in prayer position in front of your heart or raised above your head.
5. Hold this pose for up to two minutes and breathe slowly.
6. Repeat on the opposite side.

> DISCLAIMER: While these techniques can be effective to promote relaxation, it is also crucial to seek support from a friend, family member or mental health professional for reassurance and guidance, especially if anxiety and panic attacks are increasing or impacting daily functioning.

Reflect: Ask yourself the following questions:

1. When do you notice feelings of anxiety or panic arise most frequently during your teaching day?
2. Have you found any techniques or habits that help calm anxious moments?
3. Have you tried any vagus nerve stimulation techniques (such as deep breathing, humming or cold exposure) to manage stress?
4. How does your body respond when engaging in vagus nerve exercises?
5. What challenges do you face when trying to incorporate relaxation techniques into your teaching routine?
6. What small, manageable mindfulness exercises could be integrated into your classroom routine to promote calm?

CHAPTER SUMMARY

- Intense teaching situations can trigger physiological survival responses, such as a rapid heartbeat, trembling or nausea. The vagus nerve counterbalances these by promoting relaxation.
- As part of the PNS, the vagus nerve regulates stress by slowing heart rate, decreasing blood pressure and facilitating relaxation when activated.
- High vagal tone reflects effective vagus nerve function and resilience against stress, while low vagal tone heightens stress reactivity and anxiety symptoms.
- Cold exposure and calming techniques like cold-water contact, ice application or cold showers stimulate the vagus nerve and help regulate the nervous system.
- Vocalising activities such as humming, chanting or singing create vibrations that activate the vagus nerve and promote emotional calm.
- Techniques like the 5-4-3-2-1 grounding method and diaphragmatic breathing redirect attention and relax the body during stress or panic.
- Combining breathwork and movement, yoga effectively calms the mind and body, promoting stress resilience and relaxation.

CONCLUSION
Your wellbeing matters

"People will never forget how you made them feel"
– Maya Angelou

Throughout this book I've shared how teaching is both one of the most challenging and one of the most fulfilling professions you can take on. Even teachers who are feeling the weight of chronic stress express that they love working with their students. But the reality is, many of you are stretched thin – juggling the needs of students who require extra attention alongside an ever-growing workload. That's where self-preservation comes in. It's not about being selfish; it's about protecting yourself from burnout so you can focus on the parts of teaching that bring you joy and fulfillment.

Throughout these chapters we've explored how chronic stress impacts the body, brain and nervous system, and how, with the right tools and mindset, you can regain control of your time, energy and focus. However, it is important to recognise that if your sympathetic nervous system has been overactive, and you are used to rushing and being on high alert, slowing down may initially feel unsafe. This is why becoming more attuned to your nervous system states is a personal journey. Through the journey of self-awareness, self-empowerment and self-regulation, I hope you've cultivated a deeper connection with yourself. My aim is to help you learn to prioritise your needs, enabling you to remain effective as a teacher in a way that feels authentic and true to you.

The strategies and habits outlined in this book are not quick fixes but a call to prioritise your wellbeing every day. By integrating these practices into your life, you can safeguard your physical, psychological and emotional resources, allowing you to show up for yourself and your students in a more impactful way. In preserving your own mental health and wellbeing, you not only thrive as an individual but also inspire your students and colleagues to embrace their own wellbeing.

Remember, the work you do as a teacher is transformative – but the most important transformation begins within you.

Take care of yourself,

Bianca
xx

References

Be You, & Beyond Blue. (2024). *National Mental Health in Education Report.* Available from https://beyou.edu.au/-/media/about/evaluations-and-research/be-you-mental-health-in-education-report-2024.pdf

Belling, N. (2023). *Stress Less: Managing Anxiety in a Modern World.* Rockpool Publishing.

Black Dog Institute. (2023). National Teacher Survey – Summary. https://www.blackdoginstitute.org.au/wp-content/uploads/2021/08/National-Teacher-Survey_Summary_FEB_2023_final.pdf

Breakspear, S., & Rosenbrock, M. (2024). *The Pruning Principle: Mastering the Art of Strategic Subtraction Within Education.* Amba Press.

Brooks, A.C., & Winfrey, O. (2023). *Build the Life You Want: The Art and Science of Getting Happier.* Portfolio.

Brown, B. (2022). *Atlas of the Heart: Mapping Meaningful Connection and the Language of Human Experience.* Random House Audio.

Brummer, J. (2020). *Building a Trauma-Informed Restorative School: Skills and Approaches for Improving Culture and Behavior.* Jessica Kingsley Publishers.

Brunzell, T., Waters, L., & Stokes, H. (2021). Trauma-informed Teacher Wellbeing: Teacher Reflections Within Trauma-informed Positive Education. *Australian Journal of Teacher Education, 46*(5), 91-107.

Cavallari, J.M., Trudel, S.M., Charamut, N.R., Suleiman, A.O., Sanetti, L.M.H., Miskovsky, M.N., Brennan, M.E., & Dugan, A.G. (2024). Educator perspectives on stressors and health: a qualitative study of U.S. K-12 educators in February 2022. BMC Public Health 24, 2733. https://doi.org/10.1186/s12889-024-20167-8

Choquette, S. (2010). *Trust Your Vibes: Secret Tools for Six-Sensory Living.* ReadHowYouWant.com

Clear, J. (2018). *Atomic Habits: Tiny Changes, Remarkable Results – An Easy & Proven Way to Build Good Habits & Break Bad Ones.* Avery, an imprint of Penguin Random House.

Covey, S.R. (2020). *The 7 Habits of Highly Effective People: Powerful Lessons in Personal Change.* Simon & Schuster.

Dib, J., Buhagiar, K., Shelton, A., Mardones, S., La Roche, S., Caulfield, H., O'dell-Fontana, J. (2024). *State of Mind Report 2024: Exploring the Mental Wellbeing of Australian Children and their Parents and Caregivers.* Melbourne: Smiling Mind.

Doan, S., Steiner, E., Woo, A., Pandey, R. (2024). *State of the American Teacher Survey: Technical Documentation and Survey Results.* RAND Corporation.

Duffy, C. (2025). School principals report rising violence, threats and abuse from students and parents alike. ABC News. https://www.abc.net.au/news/2025-03-31/principals-teachers-facing-school-violence-from-students-parents/105107536

Durham, M. (2024). Lisa O'Neill: Energy Masterclass & How To Get It, Guard It, Give It. (Episode 128) [Audio podcast episode]. *The School of Wellbeing with Meg Durham.* Apple Podcasts. https://podcasts.apple.com/gb/podcast/lisa-oneill-energy-masterclass-how-to-get-it-guard/id1586749038?i=1000665487246

Durham, M. (2024). Dr Rebecca Collie: Combined Effort & the Power of Switching Off. (Episode 132) [Audio podcast episode]. *The School of Wellbeing with Meg Durham.* Apple Podcasts. https://podcasts.apple.com/au/podcast/dr-rebecca-collie-combined-effort-the-power-of/id1586749038?i=1000672539260

Durham, M. (2024). Dr Michelle McQuaid: Good Girl Evolution & Becoming Uniquely You. (Episode 137) [Audio podcast episode]. *The School of Wellbeing with Meg Durham.* Apple Podcasts. https://podcasts.apple.com/au/podcast/dr-michelle-mcquaid-good-girl-evoultoin-becoming-uniquely/id1586749038?i=1000680993159

Ferguson, A. (2023). *The Vagus Nerve Reset: Train your body to heal stress, trauma and anxiety.* Penguin Books Australia.

Goodman, W. (2022). *Toxic Positivity: Keeping It Real in a World Obsessed with Being Happy.* TarcherPerigee.

Green, A. (2024). *Wellbeing Leadership: A New Approach for School Leaders.* Amba Press.

Healy, G. (2023). *15-Minute Focus: Regulation and Co-Regulation – Neuroscience and Connection Strategies that Bring Calm into the Classroom.* National Center for Youth Issues.

Howard, A. (2020). *How to reset your nervous system* [Video]. YouTube. https://www.youtube.com/watch?v=jwPHHsR2Y9U

Kolpak, D. (2025). *Thriving Together: A Blueprint for Flourishing Staff and Students.* Amba Press.

Li, Y., Ahn, J., Ko, S., Hwang, I., & Seo, Y. (2023). Impact of Teachers' Post-Traumatic Stress Due to Violence Victimization: Moderated Mediation Effect of Living a Calling. *Behavioral sciences* (Basel, Switzerland), 13(2), 139. https://doi.org/10.3390/bs13020139

Maguire, J. (2024). *The Nervous System Reset: Heal Trauma, Resolve Chronic Stress and Pain, and Regulate Your Emotions with the Power of the Vagus Nerve.* Macmillan Australia.

Nagoski, E., & Nagoski, A. (2019). *Burnout: The Secret to Unlocking the Stress Cycle.* Ballantine Books.

Neff, K. (2011). *Self-Compassion: Stop Beating Yourself Up and Leave Insecurity Behind.* William Morrow.

O'Flaherty, A. (2024). Thousands of Queensland teachers say reporting student behaviour is a drain on valuable teaching time. ABC Radio Brisbane. https://www.abc.net.au/news/2024-07-29/queensland-state-school-reporting-student-behaviour-teachers/104152344

O'Neill, L. (2024). *Energy: Get it. Guard it. Give it.* Major Street Publishing.

Perry, B.D. (2020). *Stress, Trauma, and the Brain: Insights for Educators – Regulating Yourself and Your Classroom* [Video, Episode 4]. YouTube. https://www.youtube.com/watch?v=nqW2Xv16bWw

Portell, M. (2023). *Trauma Informed Educators Network Podcast* (Episode #86: Emory and Henry College) [Audio podcast]. Retrieved from https://podcasts.apple.com/au/podcast/special-episode-86-emory-henry-college/id1480791597?i=1000612329453

Rodski, S. (2018). *The Neuroscience of Mindfulness: The astonishing science behind how everyday hobbies help you relax, work more efficiently and lead a healthier life.* HarperCollins.

Savill-Smith, C., & Scanlan, D. (2022). *Teacher Wellbeing Index.* Education Support.

Taylor, L., Zhou, W., Boyle, L., Funk, S., & De Neve, J.-E. (2024). *Well-being for schoolteachers.* International Baccalaureate Organization.

The Energy Factory Pty Ltd & Deakin University. (2024). *The Silent Cost: Impact and Management of Secondary Trauma in Educators (Interim Report)*.

Tolle, E. (2001). *The Power of Now: A Guide to Spiritual Enlightenment*. Hodder Paperback.

Van der Kolk, B.A. (2014). *The Body Keeps the Score: Brain, Mind, and Body in the Healing of Trauma*. Viking.

Weaver, L. (2017). *Rushing Woman's Syndrome: The Impact of a Never-Ending To-Do List and How to Stay Healthy in Today's Busy World*. Hay House UK Ltd.

World Health Organization. (2019). Burn-out an "occupational phenomenon": International Classification of Diseases. https://www.who.int/news/item/28-05-2019-burn-out-an-occupational-phenomenon-international-classification-of-diseases

About the author

Bianca McLeish is a regional Student Wellbeing Coordinator, School Wellbeing Consultant and former Teacher with more than 20 years of classroom experience. Her professional journey has been deeply shaped by a personal encounter with teacher burnout – an experience that led her to explore the transformative potential of neuroscience and positive psychology within education.

Bianca holds a Master of Education in Positive Mental Health and Wellbeing and is passionate about uncovering what helps both students and educators truly flourish. She combines her academic knowledge with lived experience to offer practical, evidence-based strategies for recovery, resilience and sustainable wellbeing in schools.

Her approach is grounded in research and enriched by lived experience. Through compassionate conversations, Bianca supports teachers in weaving stress-prevention practices into their daily routines – empowering them to navigate emotional overload, restore nervous system balance and realign with their deeper sense of purpose. Her work is a call to action: for educators to reclaim their vitality and resilience in a profession that often demands more than it gives.

When she's not supporting others, Bianca finds nourishment in travel, yoga, nature and her ever-growing stack of books. A lifelong learner, she channels her curiosity into creating sustainable solutions – for the greater good of education, and the humans who bring it to life.

www.ingramcontent.com/pod-product-compliance
Lightning Source LLC
Chambersburg PA
CBHW052052070526
44584CB00017B/2147